RUNNING TO WIN

RUNNING TO WIN

Training and Racing for Young Athletes

Brian Mitchell

DAVID & CHARLES

NEWTON ABBOT   LONDON   VANCOUVER

ISBN 0 7153 6948 2

Set in 11 on 13pt Linotype Plantin and Printed in
Great Britain by Latimer Trend & Company Ltd Plymouth
for David & Charles (Publishers) Limited
Brunel House   Newton Abbot   Devon

Published in Canada
by Douglas David & Charles Limited
1875 Welch Street   North Vancouver   BC

Contents

List of Illustrations

All photographs by courtesy of Mark Shearman

'Then there's life in it. Nay, an you
get it, you shall get it by running.'
Shakespeare, *King Lear*

Foreword

from Brendan Foster

Contrary to commonly held views running is fun. It must be, otherwise why would so many people run without ever thinking of racing. Running is the simplest recreational activity of all and it must be thought of in this light before competitive running is embarked upon. There is nothing worse than racing without preparation yet there is nothing better than racing when well prepared.

However, when the young runner becomes serious it is then necessary to find out about athletics through the school and local club. Young athletes need to be coached by someone who must be able to explain what is going on and maintain interest, enthusiasm and progress.

Enjoy your running, good luck.

Preface

Running to Win is a handbook for the young runner. Primarily, it gives practical advice, but the principles upon which that advice is founded are also explained, and important questions of attitude, motivation and purpose are examined. The book is, of course, intended for athletes of both sexes and, except where statements are specifically aimed at the male or the female runner, everything may be taken as applicable to both.

Although *Running to Win* has been written for young runners, no attempt has been made to oversimplify established truths about training and racing. It is assumed that the reader has ambitions as a runner and that he is prepared to spend time thinking.

Many theories and practices have appeared in athletics in recent years and I have attempted to incorporate the most relevant and realistic of these. I hope, therefore that the book will also be of interest to experienced runners, active coaches and parents, who may like to try out these ideas or use them to test their own.

Above all, my aim has been to help the young runner to succeed, because success can only increase the enjoyment to be gained from an exciting, demanding and valuable sport.

B. M.

1

Why Run?

Few people can see much virtue in running, particularly in running for its own sake, and assertions of the well-being and enjoyment that running brings, carry weight only with those who are already firm converts to its rigorous but rewarding discipline. Many young athletes abandon hard physical exercise as soon as they leave school, and the 'adult world' certainly does not see regular exercise as part of daily routine.

However, those people, the vast majority, who run only for the bus risk more than simply being late for work. In his book, *The Human Machine*, Sir Adolphe Abrahams, an eminent consultant and medical adviser to the English AAA and the International Amateur Athletic Federation for many years, observed that 'the human machine is often treated with a carelessness and indifference that would be characterised as criminal if directed to any inanimate machine'. In other words, people often take more care of their cars than of themselves, yet both machines easily and quickly break down, and both need regular servicing. The 'servicing' of the human or animal body is a simple matter – exercise. Without it, deterioration is frighteningly swift; when a person lies ill in bed, muscles soon waste, when he takes no exercise, the body spoils, less obviously and more slowly than with a sick person, but just as surely. Since all machines deteriorate, and since life cannot be enjoyed by someone who is ill, it is common sense to want to maintain the quality of our personal machines; the most unfit man is a dead one!

This is not a call for fitness fanatics, but such is the general attitude towards hard exercise that a little bit of intelligent opposition to the idea that physical movement is a special and exclusive activity is not out of place. All young, healthy plants and creatures are instinctively and universally admired, even by those who do nothing to promote their own or anybody else's health. There is nothing admirable or desirable, in anyone's eyes, about decay.

If the simple value of fitness is acknowledged, and if that fitness can be so easily maintained and increased, as it can by running, then – even without the impetus of competition which admittedly encourages thoroughness – you may discover, or rediscover, the uncomplicated pleasure of movement. This is the simple exhilaration shared by young horses galloping round a field, by dogs bounding ahead on country walks and by children with their constant, if undirected, energy. It is also a feeling that all athletes know and value.

A healthy machine is necessary, but it is also enjoyable to use and maintain. The benefits of running are not confined to physical efficiency, and the old adage about the healthy mind in the healthy body is, as most would agree, a wise one too. However, it is as commonly held, perhaps rightly, that competition produces less admirable human traits, and the argument for competitive running is less clear-cut.

No sweeping claims for it can be made here. Many excellent athletes are selfish and difficult people, contributing little to their jobs, families or clubs. Many athletes are weak in the parts of their lives that lie outside of their sport. Many are narrow-minded, even ignorant, and know or care little about the bigger world of society, nature, learning. Competitive sport often seems to make these people worse, rather than better, human beings, by giving them temporary success which they greatly overrate but which keeps them along the narrow line of the sporting life. Athletics is obviously no remedy for such people, not even an advantage. In the light of such examples, claims made for athletics ought to be carefully and objectively made, and such claims can be made; there are good reasons for encouraging athletics, and some of these have to do with mind and character specifically.

There is undeniable satisfaction and pleasure in doing something where progress can be measured, where comparative success or failure are made obvious, and where the benefits accrue very directly to the actor. Training is like studying; when it is done seriously, when time is set aside for it nearly every day, there is a continuing development and challenge, and the activity becomes purposeful and satisfying. This, in itself, is a good enough reason for running, but if, added to all this is sheer physical enjoyment, the freedom of going out into the country or park, or going a long way on the road (taken to its limit by men such as Bruce Tulloh, who ran across the USA), then you have an activity to be measured in terms of pleasure as well as achievement.

Even those, the majority, who do not associate enjoyment with running, and who know nothing of the freedom so compellingly described by Ron Clarke in his book, *The Unforgiving Minute*, might understand the challenge which competitive running offers. Not much imagination is needed to sympathise with the long-term planning and preparation of an ambitious athlete whose eyes are focused on the Olympic Games. Yet, for the obvious reason that not one in a hundred runners ever competes at the games, this massive and seldom realised ambition does not belong to the majority of athletes. Their reasons for running lie elsewhere, at a different level not only competitively (where a man or woman might aim to get into a county team), but psychologically. You do not have to run the 1,500 metres in 3·40 in order to know the physical sensation of running at that pace. You do not have to win a national title in order to experience the satisfaction of a

15

maximum effort. Indeed, there must be many athletes who have been publicly unsuccessful but privately as completely fulfilled as a gold medallist. They lack the physical gifts, but they have trained and raced to their full capacity, just as the champion has. The experience is free, and freely available.

If an experience nearly equal to that of the top-class athlete can be had by any athlete, training hard at his or her own level, the pleasure of belonging to a thriving club is also open to anyone. Although the social side of athletics is not often emphasised, and does not, in fact, match that of some other sports, many clubs naturally provide this fundamental pleasure of meeting with people of similar interests. Beyond the club, there may be the county or national team, where some of the same satisfaction, in belonging to a group that has formed of its own accord, may be found. But it is mostly at club level that unity is created and loyalties established. These might be thought trivial by many people, but such loyalties do exist amongst athletes in every sport, and do provide a satisfactory reason for running. It is noticeable that many men and women who have finished with competition nevertheless stay in the sport, which means in a club. It is even more obvious that sports like football, rugby and cricket create this kind of loyalty and provide the satisfaction of belonging to something worthwhile for very large numbers of people. Whatever the sport, its followers, both participants and spectators, find friendship, action and something to carry in their imaginations at the clubhouse.

There are other more tangible rewards. Many athletes have travelled the world without paying, and it is worth remembering, if you are a young runner, that the teams will gather in Moscow in 1980 as they gathered in Munich in 1972. Running will give you a strong body, a strong mind, a lot of friendship, and perhaps take you farther than the end of the road or the switch on the television.

Page 17 Brendan Foster, a supreme track artist

Page 18 (above) Set position in the sprint start; (below) David Jenkins covering the first few metres with the body lean which allows speed to be gathered

2

The Mind and Character

In his fascinating book, *Kings of Distance*, Peter Lovesey wrote of Deerfoot, George, Shrubb, Nurmi and Zatopek all great long-distance runners: 'Each developed a degree of concentration and a strength of will that made eventual supremacy the only possible outcome.' It is this concentration, persistence and strength of will, founded on enthusiasm and enjoyment and allied to a clear-sighted sense of purpose, that reveals and creates the supreme athlete.

The young runner must pay close attention to the qualities of mind that are needed for athletic success. The first and most important point is that, in the American coach Kenneth Doherty's words, 'it is not an overnight sport'. Most young athletes are ready to make an effort in a race. Few are ready to carry their efforts through months or years of training and racing, through troughs as well as crests, to a brief period of satisfaction. That enthusiasm upon which such persistence is built, the 'impassioned will', is the possession of very few people. All that can be said is, that it is necessary and that it can be found but never imposed.

The freedom of running, the pleasure in physical movement and control, the sense of being fully alive, the excitement of competition and the satisfaction of achievement, the challenge for the future and the exact measurement of the present, the inspiration from fellow-athletes – these are the sources of enthusiasm. If enthusiasm does not come from there, it will not come at all. Presuming its existence, or its growth, we may also presume that an athlete has a good chance of success, because the whole unrelenting programme will be carried through. In the words of Lillian Board: 'To me, training every night is a foregone conclusion. Training to me is a natural thing, just as natural as getting up in the morning or going to sleep at night; most athletes, true athletes, do not think of training as being the result of sacrifices.'

There can be no hurry; the fundamental condition of the body cannot be changed overnight, but it can be changed over a period of years, by intelligent, planned employment of all that is locked up in your personality. Listen, learn, persevere and perform; cultivate the twin virtues of conscience and system, which the British national coach John le Masurier, noted as essential plates in the athlete's armour. Believe that a fair measure of success can be achieved, because you don't know that it can't! Do not turn back once you have started out. The Spanish explorer, Cortes, landing in South America, destroyed his fleet so that there could be no turning back. Something less dramatic than this, but along these lines, governs the true athlete's approach to running and racing. It is best described by the word 'decision', and it is not an easy thing to come by. It has to be part of the mind and character of any athlete who intends to do more than run round on a Saturday afternoon with his club. (Running round with your club is good, but you do not need advice, help or decisiveness, to do it.)

If you decide there is to be no turning back, you will have to be ready for many difficult patches. Before he won the European 5,000 and 10,000 metres, Juha Vaatainen suffered a great deal of illness and injury, but was undeterred. A difficulty is an obstacle, no more. An injury delays progress, it does not stop it. Illness may prevent training; the training can be resumed. British marathoner, Bill Adcocks noted, 'The best athletes don't give up because their team is down. They work even harder to try and get back in the race.' So, too, with the long, demanding, yet extremely enjoyable pursuit of training.

One point is certain – that the farther along the road you get, the more confident you become and, therefore, the more able to go on. Bruce Tulloh, when he ran across the USA, observed the extraordinary adaptability of the body, so that after some forty days and seventeen hundred miles of running, all aches and pains had cleared. Similarly, the attitude of an athlete hardens under the influence of the very activity he or she is cultivating, and both desire and capacity increase. For most athletes, there is one step back for every two forward. But this need not be so, the firmness of the forward movement will restrict the backward one.

In the beginning, do one thing : take a long, thorough look at what you wish to achieve, how you think it can be achieved, and how long it will take you. Time spent on this survey of ambitions is time well spent. Even if you only want to look forward one season, that is still worthwhile. Study carefully the factors involved in long-term preparation. The general, physical basis of this is dealt with in Chapter 4, and the detailed planning of training and racing is examined in Chapter 8; here, the concern is, to consider what will aid, and what will upset, an athlete's plans.

Intelligent forethought is the foundation of success, and positive pride its creator; the thinking will map out a route, and the pride will ensure progress along that route. Intelligence, seeking and using knowledge, is a necessary quality of the successful athlete. The more you know about training and racing, the better you will be as a competitor. The more self-respect you have, the more you will stay on the route that you have worked out. It will probably help, at least at some stages of training, to have somebody else to persuade and support you, but in the end you will train and race successfully because you want to, not because somebody else wants you to.

This strength of mind and character is, perhaps, best seen in those men and women who do essentially solitary deeds, or carry essentially solitary responsibilities. Professional adventurer, John Ridgway, wrote of his companion Chay Blyth, 'The navigation and seamanship are secondary to the spirit. Far beyond the mechanics is Chay's spirit.' What the athlete sets out to do is so much easier than what men like Chay Blyth set out to do, but, at least, the genuine athlete must have some of that kind of spirit – vigorous, sane, not easily demoralised or defeated. This resolute balance, allied to intelligence, is the mixture for success.

The cultivation of this will-power, or spirit, is possible. Franz Stampfl, the most imaginative of coaches, said that, 'It is capable of tremendous development under training and stimulus, or of near extinction under neglect.' This development may not be purely mental. It is possible to train the nervous system, to nurture the reserves, to increase the body's durability. Contrarily, it is possible to deplete the nervous energy and produce a malnutrition of spirit as well as of body. All defeats tend to do this, and unintelligent over-exertion of the will can break down the physique and, in turn, demoralise the athlete; thereby he defeats himself. It is essential to accept the very severe limitations under which the animal body must work – need for sleep, rest and proper nourishment, capacity to function only within a narrow range of temperatures, sensitivity to any heavy and repeated doses of chemical fatigue. While disregarding slight signs of discomfort, learn to judge when you have started to break yourself down rather than to build yourself up. The history of the sport is littered with the bodies of men who believed that all they had to do was exert an iron will in order to succeed. Their success finally was not much greater than that of men who lacked the necessary will; their disappointments and frustrations were bigger.

Nature cannot be hurried, as Percy Cerutty, the Australian coach, often pointed out. There are no crash courses in the preparation of a runner, though the iron-willed athlete who lacks intelligence may think there are. It is when the iron will is a partner of intelligence – as in men like Clarke, Hemery, Borzov, Shorter and their kind – that athletic greatness emerges. Cultivate your physical resources: don't try and thrash them into life, or you may end up destroying them.

The pride which has been mentioned as an integral part of the athlete's character operates to make him, or her, want to carry through whatever plans have been conceived. It also operates to make the athlete want to beat other athletes. This, after all, is what the sport is about. There is satisfaction in beating a watch, there is more satisfaction in beating other runners. While this kind of pride should not become an arrogance that sees defeated opponents as necessarily inferior people, it will be a pride which, though unobtrusive, remains nevertheless stubborn, and evident to its owner. Such lack of modesty will belong to the athlete's nature. It need only function in training and competition, and even there silently. The noisy athlete does well to remember that most of the world is not listening, and the interested public applauds the arrogant competitor who leaves his arrogance behind when he steps off the track.

Finally, the young athlete would be well advised to keep athletics in its place. Be passionately involved in the activity, certainly. Exert yourself to succeed. Gain from running the massive satisfaction that running offers. Yet be a rounded, sensitive, literate human being. It is not the job of athletics to produce people who know, or care for, nothing except athletics. Keep it in its place, which will be behind your family, your concern for the general life of the world and your education. There is a kind of athlete, and a kind of coach, who is prepared to act as if athletics were life. It is not. It is a corner – and a rich one – of life. *The Times* swimming correspondent, at the 1971 ASA championships commented on his 'three days watching worried children reduced to nervous exhaustion by zealous, intense adults'. Cultivate the enjoyment. Set it firmly amongst your other interests. Leave the intense 'adults' to their own devices.

3

The Body and Fitness

by J. L. Mayhew, University of Illinois

However willing the spirit may become, it is the body that must go the distance. All sensibly designed training programmes ultimately improve the body's reaction to the physiological stress of running. That, after all, is the object of the exercise. However, ways of preparing yourself to get the best from your body can vary; what may be beneficial for the distance runner, could be a waste of time and effort for the sprinter. Certain aspects of each method of training provide greater gains along particular lines than do others. So before plunging into any training programme, each runner must evaluate his event to determine its physiological requirements (ie speed, strength, endurance, etc) and assess each training method in the light of its physiological benefits. He must then implement a programme that allows gradual adaptation of the body to the particular stress that his training and racing will produce.

Obviously each training programme must develop the runner's capacity to produce and maintain the maximum energy over the maximum distance. This is a requirement simple to state but increasingly difficult to fulfil, if only because knowledge of physiology increases year by year, as does the willingness of athletes to benefit by it. It becomes more and more important for athletes and coaches to be as up to date as possible on all the research which can help to prepare the runner for competition.

One simple and very important fact, basic to any organised training programme, is that races below 1,500 metres are mainly anaerobic, while those above that distance are mainly aerobic. This means that, during shorter events, the oxygen demand in the body is greater than the supply, and energy must be derived without oxygen present, creating what is called an oxygen debt. In longer events, the energy demand is less acute and sufficient oxygen is present to yield that energy. Without going into the complex biochemistry of energy production, this means, in effect, that you cannot do much to increase sprinting ability by aerobic training (long runs), and conversely you cannot improve distance performance on purely anaerobic training (sprints).

Apart from this basic distinction between the effects on the body of sprinting and long-distance running, which will influence training, there are other physiological facts which are of the first importance to any athlete. These are important because they give the runner an idea both of his innate physical capacity, and also of the best ways to exploit it for his particular ends, be they running 100 metres or marathons.

PHYSIOLOGICAL CHANGES IN TRAINING

Oxygen Intake Changes
Of most concern to runners is their maximal oxygen intake, or consumption. This is the maximum amount of oxygen a runner can take into his body during an all-out effort (lasting 6–10 minutes). This is usually measured in the laboratory with the athlete running on a treadmill or riding on a stationary bicycle. In order to equate runners of different sizes, the oxygen intake is divided by the body weight. High intake values are often associated with the better distance runners.

Training can increase the maximal oxygen intake by 30 per cent depending on initial fitness and the duration, intensity, frequency and type of training used. While it is true that some people who train quite hard make no improvement in oxygen intake, most runners show substantial improvement *initially*. Once a certain level, which varies from person to person, is reached, however, the gains in oxygen intake capacity are much less, if any at all, than would be expected from the amount of time and effort put into training.

To date, research has failed to prove one training method superior to another in maximal oxygen intake improvement. In other words, it does not matter whether you do 2,000 metres of continuous running in ten minutes or 5×400 metres at ninety seconds each with jogging. In either case, at the beginning of your programme, you will make *approximately* the same gains in oxygen intake when you begin training. After you have trained for several months, this relationship may not still hold true – though there are no conclusive figures on this as yet.

Certain facts are clear, however. As long as total intensity and duration are equal, a runner will gain from continuous running the same improvement of ability to take in and use oxygen as he will from interval training. Short, intense interval training (100–400 metres), may be slightly superior to longer, less intense interval training (800–1,200 metres), for improving oxygen intake, although a mixture of these might be best. Oxygen intake is not greatly improved by sprint training.

Efficiency Changes in Oxygen Intake

Although oxygen intake capacity may not change greatly, even with very intense training, the ability to make maximum use of that oxygen, and thus run faster longer, may be greatly increased by training. Aerobic capacity is, in the final event, a matter of inherent characteristics, whereas lactic acid build-up in the blood, which diminishes the efficiency of oxygenation and thus of muscle contraction, may be changed vastly by the correct training programme. As a result of his training, in other words, the runner is capable of running at a faster pace (higher percentage of his maximum capacity) without showing a build-up of excess lactic acid in the blood.

Several reports have indicated that athletes may run at 70 per cent of their maximum capacity without build-up of lactic acid in the blood. Since treadmill simulated five-mile cross-country races show runners to use approximately 70–80 per cent of their maximum capacity, extreme oxygen debt occurs only in the final sprint to the finish. However, if the runner has not raised, by his training, the percentage of maximum capacity at which he can run without producing excess lactic acid, he is forced to run at a slower pace or incur an oxygen debt sooner in the race. The latter may be termed 'going out too fast', meaning that the initial pace was beyond the steady state (where oxygen intake remains equal to oxygen expenditure), and excess lactic acid built up to hinder the remaining portion of the race.

Oxygen Debt Changes
When the demand for oxygen exceeds the ability of the body to supply it, there is said to be oxygen debt. The effect of training upon the oxygen debt is questionable.

In shorter races (100–800 metres), a runner uses energy at a rate beyond his capacity to deliver oxygen to the muscles, and the major portion of the energy must be derived from anaerobic sources. Therefore, the ability quickly to mobilise energy and resist the great quantities of lactic acid produced is more important than a great aerobic capacity. When acid affects the muscle cells their contraction becomes unco-ordinated; however, repeated subjection to this predicament increases the buffering ability of the blood so that when lactic acid is produced it is rendered non-toxic by the buffer system. In addition, it appears that the sprinter becomes more able to tolerate these acid conditions, so that he can continue to perform with rather high lactic acid concentrations.

So, since sprint (anaerobic), events require muscle metabolism changes rather than cardiovascular changes, sprinters train at rather high speeds to produce the necessary changes that will allow buffering of lactic acid and maintain neuromuscular co-ordination of movement.

Cardiovascular Changes

The most significant factor in this area is the change in stroke volume of the heart (ie the amount of blood discharged from the heart with each heart beat) with training. Research by German physiologists in the 1950s revealed that maximum stroke volume changes could be derived in minimal amounts of time using interval training. During each recovery phase the heart continues to eject blood with a maximum stroke volume while the legs are recovering from the run. When the recovery heart rate drops to about 120 beats a minute, the next run phase is begun.

While the run phase of interval training may be quite fast, it should not be an all-out sprint. In young runners who have a maximum heart rate of about two hundred beats per minute, if the interval training run causes the heart rate to exceed one hundred and eighty, maximum stimulus for stroke volume is reduced. This is because the resting cycle of the heart, between contractions, is so short that the maximum amount of blood cannot fill the pumping chambers and maximum stretch on the ventricles (bottom half of the heart) is not achieved.

No less important is the recovery phase of interval training; if the athlete rests too long between runs, the capillaries in his leg muscles begin to close down, the stroke volume stimulus on the heart is reduced and, generally, he cools off. Therefore, maximum benefits from interval training are gained if the resting phases are kept as short as is possible to achieve about 70 per cent recovery (this is usually when the heart rate has returned to one hundred and twenty).

29

The improvements in stroke volume with continuous training are less well documented. Many physiologists assume the amount of blood pumped by the heart to be the limiting factor in maximal oxygen intake. This is based on the observation that once maximum stroke volume and heart rate are reached, oxygen intake fails to increase.

Respiratory Changes

There is no clear-cut study showing that training increases the vital capacity of the lungs. Several studies have revealed that athletes have larger lung capacities than non-athletes, but no one is willing to say if this is a training effect or due to innate differences.

The work of breathing a given volume of air is inversely related to the lung capacity. In other words, the larger the lungs, the less work required to breathe a given amount of air. In addition, for breathing a given volume of air, the energy expended by the trained and the untrained runner is the same (assuming the lung sizes are the same). However, at a given oxygen intake, or speed of running, ventilation volume, or the work of breathing, is less for trained than for untrained runners.

Although respiratory factors probably do not limit the runner's maximum exercise capacity, training appears to improve the proficiency of moving air in and out of the lungs. In a well-trained runner, fatigue in the legs rather than in the respiratory muscles probably sets the limits of performance.

Body Temperature Regulatory Changes

Heat is probably the runner's worst enemy. If he were not able to rid himself of the heat produced during exercise, great physiological damage would occur. Fortunately, when a runner begins exercising, compensatory mechanisms enable him to rid his body of the heat that results from the production of energy.

The heat regulatory centre located in the brain maintains body temperature at about thirty-seven degrees Centigrade. When exercise begins, this limit is reset to a higher value by this thermal regulatory centre so that the body does not have to dispose immediately of such great quantities of heat. Since the main heat-dissipating mechanism is increased blood flow to the skin, the raising of the temperature limit in the body allows more blood to go to the working muscles and less to go to the skin. In addition, if all the heat were delivered to the skin, great amounts of sweat would have to be produced to be evaporated, and dehydration would result.

Some research indicates that the higher temperature in the body during exercise is beneficial. The higher temperature in the muscles promotes the unloading of oxygen from the red blood cells. Resistance to blood flow is reduced by the elevated temperature, and movement of metabolic products to and from the working muscle tissues may be enhanced.

It should be noted that internal body temperature is independent of the environmental temperature. A runner does not warm up faster because it is a hot day, he just feels as though he does! Through training he will note that he begins sweating quicker than when he was untrained, but this early sweat production precedes the increase in internal temperature and only prepares the body for the run to come.

Biomechanical Changes

Most athletes recognise running style. There are some marked differences between the gait of trained and untrained runners. The running stride may be defined as a cycle beginning with foot contact and terminating when the same foot again strikes the ground. This cycle is subdivided into the support phase, when there is unilateral weight bearing by the foot, and

31

forward recovery, when the foot leaves the ground and travels forward.

Trained runners tend to lift the knees higher when running. This means that the lower leg is extended forward a greater distance before contacting the ground. Thus at a given speed, while trained and untrained runners have almost the same stride *frequency*, the skilled runners have greater stride lengths. As the pace of the run increases from slow to moderate, the athlete increases his stride length rather than his stride frequency. If further increases in speed are required (moderate to fast pace), the athlete increases the frequency of stride rather than the length. If an artificial stride length or frequency is forced on the athlete, it results in greater energy cost (higher oxygen intake and heart rate) than the stride length and frequency freely chosen. For a given speed, a runner is best left to find the ratio of length to frequency of stride which is most comfortable for him.

At the slower speeds of middle distance running, the effect of arm motion is somewhat altered from that of sprinting. In sprint running, the arms move in a forward-backward plane with a great range of motion. As the speed decreases, the range of arm swing is reduced and counter-balancing of leg movement is achieved more by the shoulders. But remember that excessive movement in directions not contributing to straight-ahead velocity may reduce your efficiency and increase your energy cost of running.

In a recent study of university cross-country runners, it was noted that while their maximal oxygen intake did not change with a season of training, their stride mechanics were altered. An increase in stride length and a decrease in frequency were noted for the better runners after training, while the opposite, shorter and more frequent strides, occurred in less skilled runners. This may mean that the more skilled athletes were able to run more efficiently, thus using less oxygen to do the same amount of work.

SUMMARY

The body is a complex machine. In training, the runner must carefully evaluate his event, judiciously select his training routines, and prudently apply his training stimulus in order to get the maximum benefit from it. Distance running will increase oxygen intake capacity in the early stages of training. Fast running will teach the body to withstand the fatigue associated with the production of lactic acid and will be of particular value to those who race in the 100–800 metres range. Interval training increases heart capacity. Development of a skilful running technique will allow more efficient use of the resources created by training. Only through sensible, planned training can a runner hope to achieve his physiological potential.

4

Quality and Quantity in Running

Training, we have established, should be regular, balanced, and geared to the demands of the race. 'Regular' can mean anything from two days a week for the very young to six days for the eighteen-year-old; it does not necessarily mean often, but it does imply that a young runner, seeking success, however slight or local, should begin to make training a part of the week's routine. The quantity, measured in terms of time spent training, is likely to be an hour (two runs of a half hour each) for a novice, two to three hours for a sixteen-year-old, and four to five hours for an eighteen-year-old, remembering that 'a little a lot is better than a lot a little'.

Variety and balance are key points in successful training. Whatever your racing distance, numerous sessions of jogging would create a useful level of fitness, just as numerous sessions of sprinting would develop strength and speed; but these types of running are not enough *on their own*. A proper training plan includes different speeds: jogging, trotting, maintaining a pace that demands effort and a fairly open stride, running hard, and sprinting flat out. Moreover, such a plan will balance these speeds, so that the body is put through a complete range of movement and every aspect of fitness is given attention.

This balance is, to some extent, governed by the distance you aim to race, for the 400 metres runner will do more fast running than the cross-country runner, as the latter will do

Page 35 (*above*) 60m sprinters gather maximum speed on an indoor track; (*below*) split-second timing in the baton-change during a 4×400m relay

Page 36 (*above*) The sprint hurdler attacks the hurdle; (*below*) and drives hard across it with the leading leg

more steady running at below-maximum pace. Within the regular, varied training, there must be particular attention paid to the demands of your own competition distance. Whilst this point is examined more closely below, it may be helpful here to describe the types of session that can be devised.

Firstly, there is the long, steady run. What is 'long' will depend on the age and fitness of the athlete. A mile is long for a girl until she has had some months' training; three to five miles is long for a boy with, perhaps, three or four competitive seasons behind him. The aim should be, to maintain a pace which, in the early weeks of training, may be not much more than a jog and which may have to be broken by short walks. Gradually this can be pieced together, until twenty to thirty minutes continuous running can be achieved.

This type of work should always be within the capacity of the athlete, so that it can be kept going without a build-up of really uncomfortable fatigue. It is probably the most effective kind of training for the young middle- and long-distance runner, and it is certainly the most natural. Long, steady runs play their part in the plans of the short-distance track runner, too, though there will be more emphasis with these athletes upon fast work.

Secondly, there is what can be called a 'trek'. A trek is an enjoyable way of exercising and, at the same time, introducing running that is above steady pace and which, therefore, puts more strain on the muscles and consequently upon the whole system. Even the very young athlete may tackle a trek of as much as an hour, whilst for the older athlete two hours or more is possible. The trek may contain a lot of walking in the early stages of training, and will do so even when the athlete is fit and strong.

The purpose of a trek is, then, to give the body an extremely thorough work-out, through a complete range of speed from walking to sprinting. Whilst it is not a rigidly planned session, it does have a distinct pattern, partly governed by the athlete's intention to go through the full range of speeds, and partly by the nature of the ground. Thus, each trek ideally, comprises about 80 per cent walking and jogging, as well as some loose, fluent striding and a few stretches of sprinting.

Wherever you meet a flat piece of ground with a firm surface, open your pace and run hard for a minute or so. Wherever you meet an uphill stretch, especially a short, sharp one, go at it with a maximum effort, keeping this to no more than forty to fifty yards. Lace all of these bits of deliberate effort together with walking and jogging, so that there is continuous movement, but movement which is constantly varied and never sustained to the point of extreme discomfort; as you become more tired do more walking and jogging, until you are within manageable distance of home, when the pace can be picked up for the final minute or two. Done over mixed country, with different routes followed every week, the trek will not only provide a high level of fitness, but a high level of enjoyment too. Like the other types of training, it cannot be relied on for complete racing fitness, but it will give an athlete much of what he or she is seeking.

Thirdly, running at or above racing pace must be part of planned training. The USA steeplechaser and Olympic bronze medallist, George Young, said of his training, 'I rarely run longer than a mile, because I can't go faster than race pace, and I believe that you have to train faster than you race.' He meant, of course, that his continuous running at pace rarely exceeds a mile; it is repeated during a training session, though a young athlete would not want, or be able, to repeat that kind of distance at speed.

The distance over which racing pace can be maintained will be established to suit the individual athlete. Racing pace, for a world-class athlete who competes over 1,500 metres, is going to be substantially under 60secs a lap. It is worth remembering that the winner of the 1,500 metres at the 1972 Olympics covered the last 800 metres in 1min 48·8secs. This is an average 54·4secs per lap, doubtless necessitating 200 metres speed below 26secs at some stage. For most young athletes this would be maximum speed over 200 metres and belongs in a speed session, not in a session of racing pace. Racing pace will, for a start, be manageable only over a distance that is less than half the race distance; that is, around 600 metres for the 1,500 metres runner, at which distance he will be able to match, or preferably outdo, his known speed for the full race distance. Again, racing pace is manageable over an appreciable distance only by an athlete who is not tired. As tiredness increases, so must the distance being run decrease.

The whole point of a specialised effort is that it must be maintained, and fluently; to labour and struggle over a pre-ordained distance may be courageous, but it makes little sense in terms of productive training. Ideally, the athlete sets himself to run at or above his current racing pace for a distance he is sure he can manage, and he then goes beyond that minimum distance. For example, late in the session, the 1,500 metres athlete, already fairly tired, runs 200 metres at pace, crossing the 200 metres mark deliberately and going on if he can. A few minutes later, he could be doing 100 metres at the same pace. Each of these racing pace stretches is followed by walking and jogging, and the whole training session should be concluded with five to ten minutes of very easy running.

It is usual, and to some extent easier, to carry out a racing-pace session on a track. As this is not always possible, the athlete can use any route that is, or becomes, familiar. The exactness of distances is not drastically important. The tempo of the fast running is, and this tempo is discovered in races. After a few races, all athletes begin to understand, not in their minds so much as in their bodies, the pace that is demanded of them, and thus the pace which they are striving to sustain. Set up the pace, rather than the distance. Then hold it for as long as you sensibly can.

There is unquestionable value in training regularly at or above your racing pace; for you are teaching the body to do what it will later have to do in the race itself. And so you are not only conditioning the physical mechanism, but also giving yourself a chance to *feel* the pace which will later be inflicted upon you. There is no advantage in entering a race, only to find that the speed being set is a speed you are not used to; training must prepare you for the strain created by a fast racing pace.

Finally, there is the pure sprint session, including hill work. This kind of training is to toughen the whole musculature, open the stride, sharpen reflexes. It puts body and mind under pressure, or, more accurately, imposes strength of mind over weakness of body and thereby strengthens both.

Absolute speed is best developed over 50, 100 and 150 metres on flat ground, and 50–100 metres on hills. There is also good reason to do some downhill running, when the slope is gentle and long. As soon as an athlete tests himself, or herself, at maximum speed, weakness is disclosed. Speed can certainly be improved, because so much of the ability to run really fast comes from the sheer strength of the muscles, ligaments and tendons. The body must be put through the fullest possible range of movement, so that it is lifted forcibly. This is a productive area of training which is too often neglected; for not only are the muscles strengthened, but the heart and lungs are worked hard during the seconds following the sprint. And there is a vigour to be derived from all-out running, which cannot be obtained from anywhere else. A part of the electric power seen in the best sprinters ought to be sought by all runners. It is got from short, maximum efforts.

A sprint and hill session will involve many repeated fast

stretches, with walk and jog recoveries, and a particularly effective method is to break these sessions into two distinct parts. Ten minutes or so of fast stretches are followed by twenty minutes of jogging and trotting, then another ten minutes of sprinting. This offers a double advantage in that the heavy fatigue of the first sprinting phase may be partially cleared during the jogging, enabling some more hard running to be done later. If the session is carried out, say, in park-land, or on a track within this kind of land, the middle part of the session could take the athlete away from the track to a completely different area, where the second phase of sprinting could be done.

Special notice should be taken of hill-running, for it is an excellent method of training, so long as it is not over done. Lifting and pushing the body uphill will create considerable strength, and it is specially important to use a vigorous arm action; this is doubly effective in that it, in turn, produces strength in the upper body, and teaches the runner the importance of a powerful drive from the arms. This aids him in fast finishes and, of course, on the hills during cross-country races. Additionally, running uphill calls for a high knee lift, a good body lean and, therefore, an open stride.

Training sessions like those outlined above will develop a high degree of both general and specific fitness; the distinction drawn here is an important one. If a young runner discovers roughly the kind of racing distance that he would like to concentrate on, then he can begin to push his training in that direction. Each athlete has to work for his particular kind of fitness within a great measure of general fitness; the one, naturally enough, helps the other.

Another point to be emphasised is, that the severity of each training session, and therefore of the whole pattern of training, must be judged and controlled. You would not go out and race every day, and neither should you indulge in training-sessions which are over-demanding. This does not mean that training is a casual affair. Effort goes into training, but effort repeated or sustained to *racing pitch* will bring the athlete down rather than build him up.

Pressure has to be regulated. This means, in practice, that the heavy and light sessions are alternated; some really top-class athletes even work to a cycle of two fairly light days to one heavy. Again it must be emphasised that what an athlete calls 'light' is only so by his very high standards. It would cripple the average citizen. A ten-mile run at steady pace is 'light' to a fit man, and a former English cross-country captain, when only able to train ten miles a day at level pace said that he was 'just managing to ward off decay'. It is still necessary to remember, though, that there is a place in all training for sessions that are well within the capacity of the athlete. Attention should be kept on the gathering effect of, say, two weeks' training, rather than on the severity of one day's efforts. The key words are: regulate, alternate, vary, and build.

Racing is, too, part of training. It should be made to contribute to increasing fitness, especially at a time of year when an athlete may not be racing seriously. Track runners use their winter racing as part of their build-up; cross-country runners may wisely use races in early season to the same end. There is nothing so hard as a race, and, sensibly used, it will add to fitness. The athlete who does not race regularly is making a mistake that is almost as serious as that of the athlete who races every Saturday. Off-season racing is simply fitted to training and may, for example, be the second run on a Saturday, a light one being done in the morning and a comparatively hard one, in the company of local competitors, in the afternoon. Athletes with little time to spare have been known to develop much of their strength from racing, though that is not recommended practice for anyone who has ambitions. Use racing to train, but do not look upon it as sufficient in itself. It is, in any case, physically and mentally exhausting, for the sprinter or the distance runner.

The training rule at all times is, 'make haste slowly'. Progress will come from hundreds of training days, purposefully and conscientiously carried out. Varied and balanced training sessions, laid alongside a planned sequence of races with the pattern and style of training matching the particular demands of the chosen race distance, will ensure gradual progress. Energy reserves and physical efficiency develop together; muscles that are able to respond to the stress of racing must belong to a body in supreme working order and whose chemical resources (for example, of glycogen) are stacked high. This condition does not come overnight.

Every athlete must decide the exact nature and amount of his running in the light of temperament, special strengths and weaknesses, personal and domestic circumstances, and specific and overall aims. Temperament leads one athlete to prefer, enjoy and thereby profit from training on a track, or to prefer, enjoy and profit from hill training; whilst both kinds of work contribute to fitness, and both should be included in all athletes' training, let some of the preference dictate what shall be done. If you prefer to take a jog the day before a race, prefer not to miss a day's training ever, then this is for you. Temperament which is destructive of proper training should be resisted, inclinations which merely persuade you to place your own emphasis can happily be followed.

So, too, with what you find in yourself physically. If your stamina is tolerably well developed but you cannot whip round a single lap of the track very swiftly, then your business may be with some fast running. If you are physically rich enough to be able to keep ticking over mile after mile, but cannot manage the short hills, some hard pushing and lifting will be needed in your plans. An early riser may favour an early-morning run which would be sheer punishment for another person. Someone whose mother cooks a family meal in the evening will need to adjust the time of his training to fit in with this. An athlete who prefers to run in company may go regularly to the clubhouse, another will visit only on a Saturday. This is all as it should be. Your job is to work out your own preferences, fit your training on to them, but do not let any of them be so commanding as to force you in a wrong direction. The truly lazy temperament does not win races and neither does the man who will not run up hills.

Training is only part of an athlete's daily routine, and that routine is, for very many people, so lacking in physical activity, that even the practising athlete is building his fitness upon weak foundations. A man who works in an office, or a young person at school, might move no more than a hundred yards, at casual walking pace, in a whole day, and this day after day, week after week. As a foundation for athletic training, the daily life of modern people – in Europe and America especially – is useless. Even the selected and deliberate hour of hard physical activity which an athlete takes upon himself may be a brittle basis on which to establish quality. Therefore, attention should be given to the possibilities offered by your private timetable.

First, where there is a chance of some regular form of exercise in addition to your running, take it. A half hour giving the dog a walk, throwing a ball about, playing squash, or simply digging the garden, may constitute a vital part of the search for competitive fitness. Certainly, the athlete who creates a second period of exercise for himself each day will be a yard or two ahead of the one who does not – especially if it is markedly different, physically and mentally, from the primary training. This is where something like circuit training contributes and a game, however casual, is invaluable. Walking, especially fairly difficult walking over country or on hills, will always assist a plan of training. The one point to remember is that this exercise should be mobile rather than static; all exercise is mobile to an extent, but playing a game of table-tennis is more mobile and more enjoyable than, say, doing press-ups.

In general, you will be a better-trained athlete if you do more than your set schedule. If, in the summer, you can manage some really hard exercise, such as hill walking, climbing, long sessions of tennis, an hour bowling in cricket nets, basketball, or any similar activity, do so. Other exercise, like cycling and swimming, cannot be said to assist runners, but in small doses does no harm, and may well be a welcome and pleasant relaxation.

5

100, 200, 400 Metres and Hurdles Training

A pattern of training can be established by adopting a two-week cycle, within which there can be twelve main sessions, spread over six days a week. The session most similar to the race distance, should be at the core of training, and will be used six times during the two weeks, on alternate days. Call it the A session, and direct your key effort at race-pace running.

Of the other three types of session outlined in Chapter 4, the sprint and hill running will take precedence over the long, steady pace and the trek, where 100, 200 and 400 metres runners are concerned, though these other efforts must be included. There may also be some adjustment of the balance of the various kinds of training during the non-competitive part of the year. But more progress will be made by working at your specialised training than by any other means. A rest may be needed, and a change is as good as one, but the ambitious runner will feel that he wants to be doing the proper training at all times, so that even during the off-season, the athlete works at his kind of running, aimed at his distance. So, the A session is pace work, and the B session is a mixture of sprint and hill running. The C session is a trek, because it contains, still, a good quantity of fast running, and the D outing is for long, steady running, which should be productive but unstrained.

Bearing in mind this balance of session with session, and the emphasis to be given to fast running, the fortnight's pattern would be: A, B, A, C, A, B/A, D, A, B, A, C. The toughness of a particular outing must be manipulated by the individual athlete. Remembering the need to avoid too much daily pressure – *measured in terms of overall fatigue* – a session will often be shortened, or will involve a large amount of jogging and easy running. You cannot pre-determine the amount of work, because you do not know how tired you will be from the previous day. The athlete must distinguish between a rigid schedule, which he does not want, and a plan, which he must have, but can be altered without being radically disturbed.

Furthermore, the demands of serious racing have to be considered, and the pattern of training adjusted to ensure that the athlete goes to a race fresh, and full of running, not tired and with depleted resources. The whole point and purpose of training is to achieve racing success. Anything that takes that away is bad, and training 'full pelt' right up to a day or so before a race will tend to take it away.

100 AND 200 METRES

The *100 metres* athlete seeks absolute speed. The distance over which this has to be maintained is so short that the problem is not one of setting up a pace which can be sustained, it is more one of developing the fastest possible tempo, without too much looking at the length of the track or the position of the finishing line. All training must be designed to allow a violent explosion of energy. As one physiologist put it, 'The sprinter must be a spendthrift.' No holds are barred in the 100 and 200 metres competitive arena, so the same must be said of training for these distances. Innate speed is certainly greater in all of us than actual speed developed when

47

running. A man or woman can run on the spot at a faster tempo than when actually lifting and pushing the body along a track, and this suggests that the vital factor is the strength to lift the skeleton. Quickness of reflex is obviously essential, and belongs partly to temperament. Style is important, too. But it is mobile strength, founded upon the highest possible level of general fitness, which will make a sprinter.

Therefore, the A session must be devoted to the creation of this mobile strength. As the great Kenyan athlete Kipchoge Keino, says, you must *practise*. The core of the training should be stretches of 40–100 metres run flat out; the 40 metres may seem very short, but it is over that kind of distance that the athlete is compelled to throw himself into top gear, and if this particular piece of training can be done on a slight downhill slope, so much the better. At 60–80 metres, the tempo is also as high as it can be, whilst at the full 100 there will be no slackening in the mind, even though there might be a fractional slowing at the end of the stretch. This primarily important training can be done either in the form of 'winders' or 'turnabouts'; that is, either jogging or walking the bends of a track and pouring on the speed along the straights, or sprinting down the straight, then turning round and jogging or walking back. In fact, it is only a very fit athlete who can maintain 'winders' for long, since there is not much of a recovery period. Young runners should use one straight for the fast work and the next bend and straight for recovery, picking up the pace on the next bend and going hard into the straight again. Otherwise do 'turnabouts'. Between fast stretches, jog or trot, and jog or trot for ten to twenty minutes at the end of a session, for this kind of natural massaging of the body can only do good.

The basic pattern of an A session for a sprinter is: jog, run easily, stride out to warm-up; then mix sprinting and jogging for the main part of the session; then trot relaxedly and easily to finish. Within that pattern, there are many possible variations. For example, you can start with three or four full 100 metres, then come down to 40 metre dashes, or you can do a complete session of 60 metre dashes. A two-part session is valuable, where about ten minutes of walking and jogging makes up the middle of the training period, allowing fairly full recovery, after which the sprint work is repeated. The vital point is, to maintain the quality of the fast running. When it becomes laboured, heavy, and slower than you know you can do, either cut the distance of the stretches, or stop. As a session goes on, maintain speed by dropping distance and lengthening recovery. Inefficient running, tired running, is not the sprinter's aim. Strong, skilful, running at maximum speed is.

The pure sprinter's sprint and hill training will give variety to his general training routine, mostly by taking him away from the track. Careful selection of the place where this training can be done, and of an interesting, varied route to that place, will add spice to the session. The pattern of training is very similar to the A session, except that hills are being used, in addition to firm, flat surfaces. The stretches employed should be short. A hill of 40–50 metres is plenty; longer ones are not for sprinters. A hill *circuit* is the most enjoyable and effective context for this session, where, say, a figure '8' is devised, containing two uphill pieces (the cross-pieces of the '8') and the remainder downhill or flat. The uphill is done fast, the downhill and flat at no more than a jog. Preceded, and followed, by a lengthy piece of easy running and a series of short sprints, this hill work is essential and rewarding. The pattern here is: 10–15 minutes trotting; 6–8 short 'turnabout' sprints; 5–10 minutes trotting; 6–8 hill circuits; 15–20 minutes trotting. This gives about an hour of persistent exercise, with up to twenty short, hard stretches.

The third and fourth kinds of training – the trek and the long, steady run – are, for the 100 metres runner, less important than sessions A and B, as outlined above; but they are important, and must be done. In addition to the very high degree of general fitness which is obtained from long, sustained physical work, there has to be both change and rest from the concentrated speed work being carried out seven or eight times in the fortnightly pattern. To a fit athlete, whatever his racing-distance, neither steady running nor mixed-pace treks are difficult, physically or mentally. The steady work is well within the limits of tolerable effort, and the mixed pace has been accurately described as getting tired without feeling tired. These sessions contribute positively to general fitness, and also ensure relief from the rigours of specialised training. They should, nevertheless, last from twenty minutes minimum (steady work) to an hour maximum (trek), though in the non-competitive months, the specialised training of the A and B sessions can be cut back for a while, and the other two types of outing extended.

One or two warnings might be offered to young runners here, applying to the pure sprinter and, more especially, to middle- and long-distance runners. The examples of sprint and hill sessions outlined above are the kind of training to be aimed at, not directly to be achieved. That it can be achieved, and improved on, there is no doubt. But the road to it is fairly long: 'make haste slowly'. That girls, in general, will be able to do less than boys is also true, so far as both the quantity and quality of running are concerned.

There is no real problem here, however. You have one absolutely reliable guide to the amount of training you can do, and that is your own body. The limitations upon the human body are, in fact, very severe; they may be found by testing them. 'How many fast stretches should I do?' becomes, by all practical tests, 'How many fast stretches can I do, without losing very much speed, and without giving way too easily to discomfort?' Your nerves will tell you what to do. They burn when the body is under stress, and then you must remove that stress.

The point made in Chapter 4 can safely be made again: assess and control the overall fatigue caused by a training session, both during and after that session, *not* by continually thinking about it, but by feeling it. Week by week, the limits will extend, until you reach the state where all fatigue is quickly shed, and even the highest levels of discomfort no longer hurt as they once did.

However, always leave the heroics, the willingness to push on to exhaustion, to the race. You have to be able to ignore your shrieking nerves when you race, but that is why you should not race too often. That kind of high-level effort is not so easy to recover from. Save it up for the occasions that matter. Here, again, is a strong reason for mapping out, balancing and controlling the pattern of training and racing.

The training requirements for *200 metres* are essentially no different from those for 100 metres, though the racing is, inevitably, more arduous and demanding. The racing tempo of the top sprinters varies only fractionally between the two distances. That there is some difference between these events can be inferred from the fact that athletes sometimes possess an apparently greater ability at the one distance than at the other, though this may be as much mental as physical. There is also the observable truth that a relatively unfit sprinter will be loath to tackle 200 metres, knowing instinctively that the demands are greater, the build-up of fatigue more fierce and hurtful.

The 1972 Olympic champion, Borzov, however, could compete in both events with consummate skill. This is because the runner has not only developed his absolute, mechanical speed, but also has taken his general fitness to the highest possible level. This is a vital factor not only in tackling both sprint events, but also in enabling an athlete to go through the preliminary rounds of competition and contest the final without the slightest loss of speed.

Such running can only be achieved by an athlete who does

much more than pure speed work, and this all sprinters must do; the 200 metres runner has a special need here, though if it differs at all from that of the 100 metres runner the difference is small. Both must spend a lot of time running easily. Few sprinters are ready to face this. Those who are, will succeed.

The 200 metres athlete should include, in his A and B sessions, the kind of fast running which is called 'tempo running'. This is fast, sustained movement, pretty well up to maximum pace, fluent, relaxed and maintained for something beyond 100 metres. Mixed with the short, absolutely fast stretches, and surrounded by large doses of jogging and trotting, this work will take the 200 metres athlete where he or she wants to go.

400 METRES

As we come to the *400 metres*, we begin to enter different territory, where pure speed, though still crucially important, is not the clearest deciding factor. It may be possible to run a 50secs lap on a basic speed that does not exceed 12·0/24·0 secs for the 100/200 metres. Speed now begins to be deployed, spread over the distance, and, therefore, held back. The 400 metres will be run in a series of virtually invisible phases, and the athlete may never actually use his absolutely maximum speed; he will slacken, in order to sustain.

The most effective kind of training for 400 metres then, is not that which concentrates too heavily on short, very fast running. There must be pure sprint work, certainly, because it develops the energetic reflexes and the muscular toughness which is essential and which cannot be gained from any other kind of training. But the body is going to have to keep up very intense and exhausting movement for 50–55 seconds, and the kind of fitness obtained from pure sprint work is insufficient to ensure this. As with 200 metres running, the general resources of the body have to be developed, and this

Page 53 (*above*) Running each lap in less than 67secs, these Olympic finalists display fluent, determined running in the 10,000m; (*below*) relaxed, alert runners share a fast pace out on the road

Page 54 (*above*) Dave Bedford shows that even the largest cross-country fields string out behind those who are running to win; (*below*) only the leading leg enters the water as these steeplechasers drive through the water-jump

development will come from a shifting emphasis, away from pure sprint work and towards tempo running, steady running, and the trek. Speed work cannot be neglected, it simply plays a different part in the overall pattern.

All distances up to, and including, the full 400 metres are valuable training distances for the 400 metres specialist. Concentrated, specialist work is done over 150, 200, 300 and even 400 metres; very fast running at 150 and 200 metres, fast running at 300 and 400 metres. The longer the stretch, the harder is the effort. The A session for 400 metres runners should contain just this specialist work, and a lot of relaxed, easy running and jogging. The fast work begins with the longer stretch – 400 metres run rhythmically and hard, but just below the threshold of total effort – then comes down through 300, 200, 150 metres, to very short bursts. There is little point in doing the series the other way about, because that brings laboured running over the longer stretches, when the athlete is already quite tired.

The pattern of these main sessions may be juggled, for example to create a 'pyramid', working from 100 up to 400 metres and down again to 100 metres.

There is no magic in this kind of routine, but it provides variety, which is good, and a definite aim, which is also good. The main thing is to carry out, regularly, repeated fast running, most of it below the full distance, so that it can be at or above the racing-pace. The ability to hold that pace over the full 400 metres comes from many weeks of training.

Hill and sprint work keeps its place in the training of a 400 metres runner, with short hills and fast running. And there must be plenty of easy running in this session as in the trek. This matter of easy running, or trotting, remains very important. The serious A sessions are arduous, mentally and physically, and a young runner will not benefit from doing arduous training constantly; there is a place for comparatively light training, just as there is a place for no training at all. You are conditioning yourself, not trying to prove a melodramatic point about how much torture you can endure.

As is often said but seldom understood, 'train don't strain'. Train hard, but train intelligently. The D session, of steady running, need be no more than half pressure for the 400 metre runner. This flushes the system and exercises every part of the body without creating heavy fatigue. A young athlete might develop this session to where it lasts between a half hour and an hour, and will probably find that it is most enjoyably done over country or parkland, and failing that on the roads.

Age and strength will indicate how much training can be done by the ambitious young 400 metres runner. To give one or two examples: an active fourteen-year-old boy, with an interest in other sports and with an education to take care of, could be satisfied with three sessions of training – a specialist track session, a fairly well organised trek with several good-pace stretches, and a steady run of about a half hour. A girl of the same age could follow the same pattern, within her own capabilities; she is, inevitably, unable to do as many fast runs, or such a long run, though she could valuably do a half-hour third session by breaking it into parts, say three ten-minute stretches at steady pace, with a walk recovery after each.

You may find, from day to day, that your capability varies and you do more or less than you set out to do. This does not matter. What does matter is that the pattern is kept going, and that you do not give up too easily. An older athlete – say at seventeen or eighteen years old – may be happily carrying through a full six-session week, alternating the A work with the other kinds of running. If this is the case, then a regular slackening of pressure is advisable, with a very easy twenty to thirty minutes of running coming in once a fortnight.

HURDLING

The athlete who takes up *hurdling* must, of course, add technique to his running fitness. Apart from this fact, which inevitably involves training over hurdles, his running will be as for the 100 and 200 metres runner. The special edge of strength and suppleness needed by a hurdler can best be got from hurdling. When it is not possible to hurdle, as is often the case in winter, then the basic running training goes on, and the gymnasium may offer facilities for specialised movement.

That special fitness (to lift and bend the body at speed) can be gained primarily from running hard over hurdles, at least six at a time. Fewer than that often looks good but the routine is not exacting enough. The only reason for using fewer would be that the runner is working at his stride pattern, from the starting line to the first hurdle, for example. Even here, the realistic thing is to go beyond the single obstacle, always reproducing a situation that very closely resembles the race.

The hurdler's A session should be devoted to very fast running, mixed with jogging and easy running. It is at this kind of tempo that the proper fitness for the event will be gained. The pattern of the remaining sessions exactly matches that of the sprinter. An accomplished hurdler is, after all, a clever sprinter, with developed control and suppleness.

6

800 and 1,500 Metres Training

A pattern of training should be established for the 800 and 1,500 metres, as for the 100–400 metres range but with its own particular features. The really specialised A session underpins everything, and is balanced and amplified by the sprint and hill work, the trek, and the long, steady runs.

As the competitive athlete begins to move away from those races that demand absolute or near-absolute speed, towards the longer events with their sustained but restrained pace, so the training effort must begin to change. Time and effort spent by a 100 metres runner on sprinting will be spent by an 800 metres runner on very fast running over somewhat longer distances. He cannot neglect sprinting though, because the tempo of the 800 metres remains very near to maximum pace, with the start and finish very fast indeed. So the runner specialising in this middle-distance race has to be nearer to a sprinter than to a distance runner.

Again, the emphasis for the 1,500 metres specialist shifts very slightly, with the intensive work carried out over, say, 800, 600, 400 and 200 metre stretches. At all times, the persistent background running for long periods of time (a better measurement than mileage), must be established and improved. The additional E session of easy running is, too, extremely productive of the kind of fitness which 800 and 1,500 metres runners are seeking. Indeed, this E session would be part, too, of the sprinter's commitment, but that is a difficult point for all but the most ambitious young runner to accept or carry out. After all, race-horses always go for an early-morning trot.

800 METRES

Presuming a reasonable level of general fitness, from which serious training can be started, the amount of hard running that an individual athlete can absorb must be discovered. A formal session is the only way. A sixteen-year-old girl athlete, aiming for the 800 metres, and with some months of training behind her, could probably jog steadily for ten to twenty minutes; then run 300 metres forcefully and fluently (which will be at 800 metres racing pace, or better – the time does not matter, the effort does); then walk and jog for a couple of laps, and come back for another 300 metres; then walk and jog once more, and come back for 200 metres at a good pace. One more repetition of the recovery phase and a final hard 200 metres would be enough. The runner may begin to struggle and slow on this second 200 metres. If she does, she begins easy, relaxed running, preferably away from the track, and keeps this up for ten to twenty minutes; if she is still running fluently and strongly after 2×300 and 2×200 metres, she can do another one or two 200 metres, followed by the long, easy running. At the end of this easy running, she returns to the track for a series of 'turnabout' sprints over no more than 50 metres.

Such a session allows the runner, and in most cases the coach, to decide practically and accurately how much of the specialised A session work can be managed. There is no point at all in trying to guess, or theorise. Go out and do the session, so that you know!

The first principle behind the training imagined for this sixteen-year-old athlete is that fast, sustained running makes the core of her session, but that there is room for, and need for, plenty of steady and easy-paced running, and for some sprinting. The fast running is done over distances that allow tempo to be *above* racing pace; ability to sustain good pace over the full 800 metres will come from weeks and months of regular, planned training. Longer, and inevitably slower, stretches – say, 400 and 600 metres – can occasionally be included, but are, at good pace, too exhausting to be really valuable for someone at this level.

The second principle to govern these main sessions is, that the overall amount of fatigue they produce must be taken into account when the other sessions are being planned. This kind of track training is not easy, and that is the reason for making the A session an alternate-day session. Variety is necessary and other kinds of physical conditioning have to be taken into account; but, above all, concentrated mental and physical work like this specialised track session cannot be done every day.

Around the A session, whatever its content in terms of the number of fast stretches run, the rest of your training has to be built. This, for the 800 metres runner, means good quality sprint and hill sessions, thorough and thoroughly enjoyable treks, and steady running which should never degenerate into a plod.

The sprint and hill training can be done along the same lines as that described in Chapter 5, for 100 and 200 metres runners. The difference between 800 metres training and sprint training does not lie in this specialised fast work, but in the A sessions. The trek, too, may be given a particular emphasis by the 800 metres, and 1,500 metres, runner, with somewhat longer stretches of good-pace effort, not as long or as hard as those done on the track in the A session, yet good efforts that teach maintenance of pace. Again, this C session differs essentially from the A session, because it is done away from the controlled environment of the track, there is a complete variety of pace and distance, and the runner deliberately pulls out before excessive fatigue builds up. It is not an easy session, rather it is free, varied, and compelling exercise that lasts much longer than either the track sessions or the most extended race undertaken even in the cross-country season.

Regular, prolonged running, at a pace that can be maintained without extreme discomfort, but at which the body is getting hard exercise, is the other vital ingredient of the 800 metres runner's training plan. With the young athlete, age and fitness must dictate what is a sensible and productive quantity, and this will lie between twenty minutes' and an hour's running. It is often forgotten just how exhausting even twenty minutes of continuous running can be, and also just how valuable is the training effect of this sort of work. No single type of session is more profitable than maintained pace. This should be understood, and will be by any athlete who goes out and does this basic and clear-cut exercise. Over the weeks, months and years, the steady-running session can be developed, so that by the time the athlete is a senior, mature and strong, a full hour's hard effort can be pursued, still without running into exhaustion.

So, the four sessions – A (specialist track work), B (sprint and hill), C (trek), and D (steady pace) – can fall into the same pattern as the sprinter's: A, B, A, C, A, B/A, D, A, B, A, C. And do not be afraid to ease down on any single session if the residue of fatigue from a previous session is still too much in evidence. Rest is a good word, not a bad one, so long as it is the exception in your training, rather than the rule.

1,500 METRES

This general, fortnightly pattern applies to 1,500 metres training, too. The A session will then be given a 400/300, rather than a 300/200 metres emphasis and this kind of work will both compel and allow a further development of easy and steady running, in the remainder of the A session, as well as in the other sessions. However, there is not a lot of difference between the running needed by a 1,500 metres runner in training, and that needed by the 800 metres specialist; natural talent, stemming from physique, temperament and style will make the difference in race ability.

This is *not* to say that there need be no difference between the methods of training, but rather to point out that, once the slight shift in the balance of specialist effort has been made, the difference in competitive performance comes from the established physique and character of an athlete. If an athlete were racing at both distances regularly, but concentrating on, say, 1,500 metres A sessions as suggested above, it could still happen that he was successful racing at 800 metres if that were where nature was directing him. Finding success, and ability, at the shorter distance, he would, then, be well advised to run those 300 and 200 metre stints, thereby getting the benefit of both his natural talents and his conscious efforts.

It is worth emphasising yet again that though the length of fast stretches in the 1,500 metres runner's A session may seem too short, they are long enough for the young runner – certainly for the under-sixteen boy and the under-eighteen girl. It is advisable to keep the distance covered in fast training down for a year or two at least. The occasional two- or three-lap run, at a good flowing pace, is very useful, but it cannot form the basis of a young athlete's main training effort. That kind of training comes later.

Trek training for the 1,500 metres runner, as in 800 metres training, allows some good pace to be achieved over distances of 200–800 metres, with the usual and valuable easy running, some jogging, sprinting and short hills. This provides a very thorough work-out, blending pace and continuous exercise. The D session of steady running should also last between twenty minutes and an hour – a fluent, relaxed, continuous effort, and never just a plod.

With a long off-season period, in Britain, at least, the specialist track runner must consider using the over-distance running offered by cross-country competition. This is valuable work, providing a change from training, toughening the physique, keeping the athlete in touch with racing, which is, after all, what athletics is about, and presenting a few targets at which to aim during seven months almost complete absence from the track. These days, with 'all-weather' tracks in various parts of the country, and even with that rare building, an indoor track, to be found, it is possible for an athlete training for anything in the 100–1,500 metres range to get a few winter races; but, generally, the middle-distance runners have to rely on cross-country races. This is not any disadvantage; you can still train for your specialist track distances, taking in the cross-country as you go. A fit athlete in full training will find himself in the front half of most cross-country fields anyway, and, not being ambitious in this direction, will not suffer disappointment if races are not won. This kind of Saturday race becomes, in effect, a steady-running session. It puts you in touch with club and school teams and a different bit of land to run on. The cross-country run will not slow you, because it is never more than a sixth of the overall training plan. Running over rough surfaces, which throw a runner off balance and compel a slightly higher knee lift, breeds yet another degree of strength, which can only be good for the following summer.

One final, special point must be made, about the amount and kind of 800 and 1,500 metres training which girls can, or should, do. The yard-stick, as before, is whether the training can actually be absorbed and enjoyed. Experience in recent years has shown that girls can train and race regularly and hard, and do long runs and formal track sessions. It must be said though, that an individual athlete should resist having a crash course of hard training forced upon her. Find the coach who will talk about this with you, who will help you to devise the training that is right for you as an individual, as well as right in principle and pattern. And have the patience to develop your training very gradually and deliberately, making it harder and longer as the months pass. That is the only way to success.

7

Longer-distance Training, including Steeplechase, Road and Cross-country

'Longer distances' are those above 3,000 metres or 2 miles. Girls will generally compete in the two to three mile range, boys between two and six miles. Under AAA laws, nineteen-year-old boys may run up to 35 kilometres, that is nearly 22 miles. The English Schools' AA championship cross-country event for those between sixteen and eighteen, is over 5 miles. If they compete for a club, boys aged between seventeen and nineteen years may run up to six miles, and those aged between fifteen and sixteen up to four miles. On the track, there is a 5,000 metres event for the senior group at the national schools' championships, whilst the occasional 10,000 metres can be entered. Steeplechasers run either 1,500 metres (youths), with 13 hurdles and 3 water jumps, or 2,000 metres (juniors), with 18 hurdles and 5 water jumps. Nevertheless, longer distances are regularly tackled by young runners, and it might be remembered, though not copied too often, that a thirteen-year-old Canadian girl has done a marathon in 3 hours 15 minutes.

Although there is this fairly wide range of competitive distance, and an even wider range of mileage done by young athletes in training, the practical approach to distance running can be founded upon the fact that we are here talking about

65

'sustained good pace', a kind of determined D session. It follows that the most effective training is that in which good pace is kept up. The speed is, inevitably, below maximum, but should be maintained over a distance similar to the racing distance. There is still an argument for pushing training pace above racing pace, but the need to keep good pace going for between ten and thirty minutes is becoming the vital issue. Between hard training and hard racing, the tempo changes, certainly, but the change is not great. Therefore, raising the pace in training is not a major consideration, whereas maintaining it is.

The A session work must be more than 'steady', but not a lot more. Sustained 'sub-maximal' running is the most successful means of improving the circulatory system, which is the body's most vital mechanism as far as the distance runner is concerned. The longer your racing distance, the greater its importance, and so the greater the need for that kind of training which improves the quality and co-ordination of heart, lungs and circulation.

The ideal A session for the distance-runner, always remembering that this session is about one-half, or probably less of the complete training routine, is a few miles of continuous running. Continuous running does not necessarily mean running at an unvaried pace; it should, however, exclude both walking and jogging, though the latter may, inevitably, occur. The natural way here is the right way. The runner sets off in a relaxed fashion, moving loosely, well within his capacity. After a mile at this pace, the pace is taken right down, for a minute or two; it is increased again, gradually and you begin to roll along, putting an effort in now. This phase will last from ten to twenty minutes, when the main work is done. With a really good sweat on, and becoming increasingly tired, you hold on for a few minutes, then ease right down.

After a few more minutes, the pace can be allowed to

increase, but it will be much slower than it was during the main phase. Running now at a recognisably steady tempo, and turning for the last mile or two towards home, you can put in regular bursts – not sprints, but fast stretches, still fluently carried out and lasting no more than one or two hundred yards. Each of these is followed by a short, very slow jog. In sight of the finish, say about a half mile out, pick up a good pace again, which will by now be quite hard work; take this all the way.

Such a session will take up to forty minutes. That is well beyond the duration of a distance race. It will, of course, vary according to the amount of easy running done at the beginning and end; just as the duration of the good-pace stretch will vary from person to person, and day to day. This is immaterial; the important point is that the right *kind* of exercise is being taken. In time, and naturally, the quantity can be built up.

Place this A session, therefore, at the centre of your training. Do it on country, road or track, as conditions and inclinations allow. They all have their merits as training surfaces. The grass and mud of the cross-country route is a surface that forces the athlete to lift his feet, and therefore his legs, and so to work fractionally harder than on a firm surface for the same speed; this is effective training. Also, the body is thrown slightly by an uneven surface, and that, in turn, makes the process of running more difficult, which is good. Road and track allow fast running, but the athlete must be careful on the very hard surface of the road. Above a steady pace, there is liable to be injury; sprinting is positively to be avoided.

Next to be considered is the overall pattern of training, with the A session as the foundation. This pattern should be slightly altered from that of the 100–1,500 metres range, and the best arrangement is: A, D, A, C, A (or D), B/A, D, A, C, A (or D), B. The A session is occasionally replaced by the D (long steady) session, because the former can be very exhausting. It is useful sometimes to take the pressure off, and this long, steady effort is, as has already been stated, invaluable to the distance runner.

The B session remains important; hill work should be a regular part of all training. Although very fast running gives a muscular toughness that cannot be obtained from any other kind of running, range of movement is the key here. Lifting the body uphill, with a strong, driving arm action, will condition your muscles, while high level of fatigue created by this intense work will improve your ability to withstand this tiredness. The flat stretches will be easy! So run them fast!

Trekking is, too, at the heart of distance training, and can eventually be done in huge quantities. A fit sixteen-year-old boy could take an hour or more of this kind of training and a girl, thirty to forty minutes of it. This kind of running, devised by the great Swedish coach Gosta Holmer, is invaluable. The English word trek has been used deliberately in this book, because it signifies a long and enjoyable piece of exercise over pleasant, mixed terrain. The benefit of this training to the distance runner lies in its continuous yet varying movement; an hour's trek, is an hour's unbroken exercise. Varying the pace is a kind of bonus to be obtained from trekking. Both stamina and speed are gradually improved, whilst the individual runner remains in charge of his particular variations.

Careful choice of route can make it an interesting excursion, not necessarily over a single circuit. There is value in turning round at the end of, say, a five-mile lap and going back again in the other direction, thereby turning all the hills round, too. A change is nearly as good as a rest, though the second five miles may be a bit more arduous than the first. Another advantage is that a group of athletes of mixed ability and age can train together over a large trekking lap, since those who wish to may pull out at the end of the first. The trek is not enough by itself, however. Not enough sustained running is done, although this training is essential as a part of the long-term pattern.

The fourth session of the sequence involves a long run at fairly comfortable pace. This is a strictly individual matter, because what is comfortable for one runner is most uncomfortable for another, and although there is drama and courage in setting your teeth and hanging on to somebody else's tempo, this is not the purpose of the D session. This part of your training plan is meant to build up the strength and the resources of your body. This is truly stamina training, but it will only be so if you run a long way. To do this, you have to run within yourself – not jogging, but running fluently and rhythmically for a half hour to an hour. Kept moving for a long period of time, the body will be under pressure, though not under strain.

If a second daily session can be regularly, or even occasionally, fitted in, it will pay high dividends. Again, it should build up, not break down; a fit athlete can take such a session, but it is not meant to be his main work.

The training described above fits the needs of the specialist steeplechaser. Fast stretches of the A session should be chosen to match the racing distance, as always, and this will mean that the specialised hard running is aimed at 1,500 metres and 2,000 metres. Therefore, stretches of 200–600 metres are repeated at sustained pace, working down from the longer to the shorter distance (for example, 600, 400, 400, 200, 200, all at pressure).

The other training should be as for the 1,500 metres 'flat', with the addition of hurdle practice and, when possible, water-jump practice. The latter is not often possible for most young runners, so a substitute has to be found. The exhausting business of raising the body on to the water jump and across the water demands special preparation; if just one steeple-chase hurdle can be acquired, the distance of the water can be marked out on the ground and clearance attempted several times, say at the end of a track session. Even a box in the gymnasium can be used in this way. If this facility simply is not available, some hurdling, at steeplechase pace, over an ordinary track hurdle suffices if it forms a regular part of at least half of your training. High leg-raising, and special stomach-muscle exercises will help the steeplechaser, as will, of course, a race whenever chance arises.

A special consideration must be brought to the attention of distance runners. Whereas, below the 3,000 metres mark there will be, for young athletes particularly, a set season, and a short one, the distance runner has the chance, and usually the desire, to get competition at any time of the year. Of course, the young runner should run winter and summer, and in Europe there is never a lack of opportunity; but while he should *run* throughout the year, he also ought to think in terms of there being one serious competitive season and a few months when there is training and occasional racing. The supreme distance runners, like Ian Stewart, do some cross-country and some indoor racing in winter. They retain, and increase, their fitness then. They do not pursue a relent-less, disruptive and exhausting policy of off-season competition. Serious racing is physically and mentally depleting and the amount of hard, out-of-season racing, should be carefully controlled.

Conditions, generally, will not allow a full sequence of specialist training in winter (though all-weather tracks are making this possible for many runners), but the pattern should be kept as near as possible to the ideal. In March or April, for all Europeans at least, genuine speed work becomes a practical proposition again, even where tracks are old-fashioned. However, large percentage of distance training can be done at any time of the year just as planned, and the athlete should be working towards his or her main competitive season. Lack of track training should not affect his race preparation; very rarely does any sportsman attempt to

Page 71 Commonwealth Games 400m gold medalist, Yvonne Saunders,
gives a superb display of control and fluency at speed

Page 72 (*above*) Total effort off the last bend; (*below*) running straight and dipping for the tape pay dividends for the sprinter in a tight finish

compete during every month of the year, even in sports that are far less physically demanding than running.

Another point of considerable importance to the young runner, and especially the young distance runner, is the distance to be covered in training. It is unfortunate that 'mileage' has become a cult word among runners; the number of miles covered in a week is, for some runners, the major consideration. It is, of course, a convenient way of summarising effort, but it is obvious that the way that mileage has been done matters, too. Ten miles in a week for a marathoner at marathon pace could be useless, whereas ten miles of sectioned sprinting – say, 150×100 metres, even spread over a week, would be a tough assignment. Most of us, even the ordinarily lethargic citizen, could walk twenty miles if we had to. Fit twelve-year-olds can run four miles at steady pace; jog and run six or more; trek a good ten; and jog and walk even farther. So, if the question of optimum, or of possible, mileage arises, as it always does when training is discussed or planned, put it in perspective.

Mileage, pace, time spent out on track or country, the kind of surface are the factors to weigh. As has been said, each individual athlete will find his or her own effective mileage. The minimum for a single session, below which the effect of training is negligible, is about one or two miles of steady pace, or a mile of mixed pace, or a half mile of sustained pace. *None* of these is recommended! The steady pace is hardly worth changing into running clothes for. The mile of mixed pace would just about stretch your legs and air your lungs. The short, sustained effort would be uncomfortable and ineffective, and you would probably pull a muscle!

SUMMARY OF TRAINING

Summarising what has been explained in Chapters 5, 6, and 7, it can be said that training must have a pattern, that this pattern covers all possible kinds of running; that the emphasis shifts, according to the race distance aimed at; and that the foundation of all training, and therefore of all fitness for racing, is a very large amount of persistent and consistent exercise.

As all intelligent athletes, young or otherwise, will want to fit their training into a normal life, and still get the maximum results from that training, two points ought finally to be emphasised. First, make use of Saturdays and Sundays, when long runs and double sessions can be done. Except when the race is an important one, use it as part of a weekend's effort. Second, make each training session a concentrated one; don't let it leak away. Make it *continuous*; too many athletes fail to keep moving. Nothing less than a fast, relaxed walk should come between the first and last minutes of a training session. If you want to stand and talk, do so afterwards. By training properly, hard and purposefully, you will have time left for the other essential parts of life.

8

The Overall Pattern of Training and Racing

Training is the means by which continual progress is ensured. Racing is the true test of progress. There is an absolute need to plan, guide and control training and racing, viewing them as two parts of one process, each guaranteed to help the other, if intelligently developed.

In planning your training and racing, several points must be pondered. How much planning is necessary? What changes will be introduced, over a long period of time? How important are facilities? When can training best be done? Are targets important? How can progress be measured? How can the off-season period be used to help the competition season? How often should a young athlete race? What lessons can be learned from racing? All these questions will influence the overall pattern of training and racing.

The training plan drawn up by an athlete, if built on sound principles and made for the individual, must be valid and effective throughout the year. Adjustments will be made, for reasons such as weather conditions, desire for variety, the particular phase of the season that has been reached, awareness of special needs (eg after illness or injury), but if a plan is right, it is right for all time. The changes that are introduced over a long period, should not be changes in pattern, but ones that effect quantity and quality. There will be an increase in time spent training, in mileage covered, and in the speed at which serious running is done.

Of these three, the last, the 'quality', offers most scope for improvement. Eventually, after several years, mileage will reach an optimum limit, as will time spent running. But it is very difficult to be sure that you have come to the point where your fast running is not improvable. The kind of strength which allows you to move very fast, and the condition of heart, lungs and blood that allows the strength to go on operating, is capable of much improvement; as it improves, so you can run faster, because you can lift and push the body more and more vigorously.

It is unlikely that many athletes find their limit here. You must, anyway, always work on the assumption that you do not know your limit, that you keep looking for it without ever finding it. When you feel that you are spending enough time on training, and covering enough mileage, remember that you always have the speed – the quality of effort – to improve. Never ignore or devalue the rest of the training, but always look for increase in this part of it. To work yourself up to running for several hours a day or fifty miles a day would be feasible, if stupid. To fling into a few comparatively short stretches of running every ounce of mental resource you currently possess – effort which does not necessarily involve running to exhaustion – and to set this as the lynchpin of a balanced programme, is to begin to take yourself towards success.

To indicate how this gradual increase in training is achieved, take the case of a sixteen-year-old 800 metres runner with a good background of training. He is able to tackle a severe track session, with fast stretches well below race distance but above race pace; and if, for example, he can manage between six and ten of these, with jogging and easy running, his aim becomes to exert greater pressure during these stretches. *Rather than increase the number, increase the speed.* To keep on reeling off, say, 300 metre stretches is good training. To increase the number of these is to increase the quality of training. But to increase the speed of running, is to increase the body's range of movement, the demands made on the muscles which lift and push the body, the stress placed upon the heart, lungs and blood circulation, and to make sure that the mind is acting its part behind all this. At the 1952 Olympics, Zatopek found the pace and the pressure of the marathon well within his capacity, even after he had run, and won, the 5,000 and the 10,000 metres, and that great athlete's training had been constructed on fast stretches.

It is true that Zatopek also gradually increased the *number* of these stretches. Indeed he increased them beyond the point where this made any training sense and the real lesson to be learned from him was the value of *fast* running which induced the high pitch of running fitness. It must be emphasised yet again that other parts, and kinds, of training matter, too. But the speed, the quality, is the part of training that needs to be attended to and developed. So, the sixteen-year-old 800 metres runner doing his 300 metre stretches fast, will intend to do them faster as the months and years go by. Keep the distance of the fast stretch somewhere near, but always below, the race distance. Keep the number of these stretches down to a figure which is manageable at speed and within the limits of utter fatigue; and above all work at the speed.

Planning emphasis upon the speed training at no point implies ignoring the other types of training, or the need gradually to build them up. Plan gradually to extend the overall time spent training, and to increase the mileage done. The point has been made though, that effective and clear-cut limits in these areas of training are eventually met.

When an athlete sits down to plan his training, he will

have to consider where this training is going to be done, and what effect the possession or the absence of ideal facilities is likely to have upon training. There is never complete freedom in this matter of a time and a place for training, though the young athlete will almost always have more choice and opportunity than the adult. Even then, training will, mostly, have to be slotted in before, between or after school, work or homework.

Each week, plan when and where you intend to train – what surface you will be on, what time of day it is likely to be, and therefore the type of session you can manage. There may be no track in your area, the dark months of winter may restrict you, you may have to travel. Firstly, plan so that as little of your time as possible is taken up by training, because enthusiasm will eventually be weakened if your leisure hours are commandeered by your running. Do as much as you enjoy, of course, and hang around the track or clubhouse if you feel like it or if you have your eye on somebody there, but do not let training become something that dominates the days.

Make full use of Saturdays and Sundays, which are the obvious days for long runs, treks, double-session training, and even treble-session training. Few athletes take sufficient advantage of the weekends, primarily because they do not plan them. For example, a group of runners can, without much difficulty, book lunch in a cheap local restaurant, and meet for morning and afternoon training on a Saturday or Sunday, using a clubhouse or local school for changing. Sitting down to lunch with friends who are also athletics enthusiasts is itself a pleasure, so the day can be very enjoyable and physically profitable. To take this a step further, as many clubs do, occasionally a training weekend can be arranged, and six sessions done in two days, with an easy jog before breakfast, a longish run in the morning, and some speed work in the afternoon. There are plenty of small hotels or guest-houses, especially in winter, that will accommodate well-behaved runners!

Although availability of facilities is important, no young athlete, least of all a runner, should be deterred by the lack of a private stadium. Many have to use the streets in winter, and that is not a serious handicap even though an all-weather track would be preferable. The most necessary 'facility' then becomes a really good pair of training shoes, of which there is no shortage. Far too much emphasis can be laid upon the need for facilities where a runner is concerned. Most other sports need special buildings and special surfaces, but the runner only needs shoes. Never be put off by rough ground, small fields or town streets which have their own floodlighting anyway.

If, then, you know what you want to do before you do it; if you know how to develop and intensify training over a long period of time; if you work out thoughtfully when and where you can run; you must then set up a line of targets. Most of the dates of major events are known well in advance and can be plotted when a review of the season's training is made. Around these important dates, the athlete settles the races, and the distances, he may want to use as a vital part of training. Clear targets make the whole business of training interesting, and they act, inevitably, as strong incentives and as means of measuring progress.

A serious piece of forethought in this matter will also serve to keep an athlete's attention on the races that matter, and place the other races where they belong. In Britain, in the cross-country season particularly, it is too easy to take a short, local view of pre-Christmas racing, and perhaps enjoy a measure of success, only to find that the big championship events, coming from January to March, are so much faster and more difficult that your performance in them is disappointing.

It is an advantage to plan towards a final, major target which will lie at the end of the road, and to remember that the quality of most other racing is likely to be mediocre in comparison with, say, a national championships. For those still at school, there will be school fixtures, district championships and county championships on the way to the biggest test of all, the national events. You may not get beyond district level, but it is still worth planning towards that. If you stop there one year, plan to get past it in a year or two's time. Keep your line of targets clearly in view. They will encourage you to train, and give you a lot to look forward to and aim for.

With a clear, progressive line of training established, it is useful to check regularly your exact physical condition. The race, of course, does this. So would a very formal and designed training session, preferably carried out in the company of your coach or adviser. This session would be, in essence, an A session, on the track, or a known circuit. A really thorough warm-up, as if for a race, would be followed by timed fast stretches, and the fullest amount of steady running that can be managed. Into the training diary goes a detailed description of this session, and you then have a yardstick against which future training can be measured. When the next formal session is held, there should be noticeable improvement, however, slight, in the speed, quantity, and ease with which the training is accomplished. Such formal sessions are not meant to replace racing, or time trials, nor are they needed more than half-a-dozen times a year. They remain *training* sessions, indications of how much work an athlete can do at a given moment.

Time trials are a special routine, to prove the degree of speed that can be achieved. A time trial is also an immensely demanding activity mentally, because it is done by the athlete on his own. Again, it is not an activity that should be overdone, because it tends to upset the training routine. But a regular, perhaps monthly, trial is a valuable part of training.

The time trial should be carried out over a distance which is considerably less than racing-distance (roughly half the race distance except, of course, for sprinters), but which allows sustained speed. As most young runners in Britain will have a chance to take part in the AAA 5 Star Award Scheme, this offers an immediate and clear-cut way of carrying out a time trial, with the special incentive of the points scheme.

Race planning is every bit as important as the planning of training, not only because an athlete wants to know exactly which races he or she is aiming for, but also because the less serious racing, often under the athlete's chosen distance, must be made to play its part along the line of planned preparation and competition. Thus, if you are looking for a serious, all-out competition every third week or so (which would be a rational distribution of effort), other races can be made to contribute to your preparation. For example, there may be school events which would demand comparatively little from a properly trained runner – would, in fact be no more than a fairly hard D session for the cross-country runner, or part of an A session for the track specialist. At school, the serious athlete can be useful to himself and to his team by racing twice in track events which are below his intended distance, and saving himself for the championship events at his distance, which are themselves stepping stones for further championships. For example, an 800 metres runner can do the 400 and 200 metres in school, and often in club, matches, without great expenditure of physical or nervous resources, because the standard is often low.

Two special points have to be made about planning the less serious racing. Firstly, this kind of racing is not true racing but is, rather, a very controlled kind of training. Secondly, during the off-season, especially for the track athlete, completely unusual racing may be attempted for variety, company and pleasure. This winter racing breaks the general rule, of course, that less serious competition should be under-distance, but you are dealing here with a competitive season which does not coincide with your own.

It has already been suggested that to race seriously every three weeks or so is sufficient, and this must be heavily under-lined. True racing is a physically and mentally exhausting process. Intelligent planning takes note of this fact, especially where the athlete is young. Develop and nurture your strength. What you do as a young athlete is enjoyable and satisfying; what you will do in later years is what matters.

Racing, whilst exhausting, should be utterly constructive. It is, after all, the final purpose of the sport, the challenge and the reward. A sprinter may thrive on plenty of racing, but even the sprinter's energy will eventually drain off. For the runners who race at 400 metres and above, there is an enormous expenditure, with the particular and obvious truth that the longer the race-distance, the deeper the exhaustion.

Control your diary, rather than letting it control you: Saturday may appear every seventh day, but that does not mean that racing should do the same, a truth generally accepted in British athletics. When you plan your racing, especially its frequency, imagine that the days do not have names, and that you do not, therefore, have to consider them in blocks of seven. Place the racing where you want it. Of course, that will most often be a Saturday, but the frequency, and certainly the intensity, of racing is fully within your control, and must be if you are to get the best from training and racing.

As the planned race is the centre of the stage, so it is something from which many of the athlete's most important lessons can be learned. In training, an athlete's physical and mental ability is never fully revealed. In racing, everything is revealed to the individual runner. Therefore, the moments of the race, and certainly the time afterwards, are the most instructive. The extent and quality of training are then put to the only test there is. Mind and character are known. It is, therefore, worth thinking about the race afterwards. Ask; was I strong enough, was it my best possible effort, is my training right, what should the next move be, in training and racing? The intelligent, purposeful runner will get answers to these questions, and the answers will lead him to the next phase of training, and towards the next race. Incentive and progress arise from deliberate analysis of your racing. And it is now that you need an adult adviser, to discuss things with you and to help your judgement. Looking back is an essential part of planning, as all students of human affairs know.

Finally, it is necessary to emphasise that the whole process of training and racing is essentially an individual matter. This truth in no way contradicts the other truth, that there are right and wrong ways of training. When the principles have been grasped – once, for example, the key physiological facts are appreciated, or truths taught by great athletes are adopted and made part of all training – then each athlete must proceed along his or her own road.

In terms of quantity, it is obvious that what is enough for one athlete at a given moment, is not enough for another, and too much for a third. Each athlete has his likes and dislikes when it comes to training. So long as the crucial truths of training are acknowledged, these individual tastes ought to be allowed for and even cultivated. Forcing a routine on somebody, or slavish copying of somebody else's routine, is neither good sense nor good living. There is also always room for experiment, so that you may find out what suits you best, and line this up for future use. One thing you should be ready to do, and that is, to learn. Find the truth about training, shape it to your purposes and circumstances, and keep one ear open for whatever the latest genius has to say.

9
The Race

There is a great gap between training and racing. Very many athletes are prepared to train regularly and hard; very few master the problem of racing – yet racing is what the sport is finally about. Full of resolve, alert, elated, intent and relaxed – that is the state of mind, ideally, in which the athlete approaches the race. The 'approach' stretches back well before the day of competition, even as far as the moment, perhaps years before, when the athlete decided to train and plan seriously. Herb Elliott said, 'The athlete's life is painstakingly moulded so that for a few seconds or minutes, on a certain day, he will be able to give his maximum effort.' Elliott used the image of a reservoir to describe this effect; training has filled the reservoir, and the runner must empty it during his race, tapping it fully, so that he finishes with all his resources spent. Filling the reservoir is difficult enough. Having the courage and the intelligence to empty it and still get across the finishing line is infinitely more difficult.

Since the intention is to bring yourself to the race in the best possible physical and mental condition, special care must be taken with training during the last few days. Mental attitude is all-important at this stage, and, in the week before, you should examine every phase of the race. It has to be accepted that 'nerves' will be experienced in the pre-race period, when the mind turns towards the event, and the race is run many times in imagination. This is not necessarily a bad thing, and, in any case, the other competitors will be undergoing similar stress. If you have trained conscientiously and if you set your mind on what you intend to do, confidence will come. If you have retained a sense of proportion and a sense of humour, you will be able to keep the event in its place in the calendar of your affairs, and still pour every ounce of directed effort into it.

Normally hard training can be kept going until three days before competition; then there has to be a definite tapering-off. Although some men have run even on the morning of a race and many train the day before, the recommended practice is to finish training on Thursday, if your race is on Saturday. No further reserves can be created at that stage. A gentle, untiring jog, like a pre-race warm-up, may be favoured by an individual athlete, but is not necessary. All that could be done has been done. Thursday's running should be shorter than usual (two to four miles with some relaxed striding), and without pressure.

The fullest possible quantity of rest and sleep is needed by an athlete at all times. Before an important race, no chances should be taken, because the chemical fatigue that swamps us when we are tired is potent enough to spoil performance. Ensure that the body is allowed to stay free from avoidable fatigue before it is required to undergo the maximum fatigue of a race. Get nine to ten hours rest if possible during the two or three nights prior to competition; this amount of rest never does any harm, anyway.

On the day of the race, try to stay relaxed, even though tension will increase. Calm concentration on what you intend to do will see you through the very difficult hours just prior to a race. This is the most wearing time, because the athlete now wants to get started, but cannot. Kit should be carefully checked and packed. Travel arrangements should allow plenty of time. If training has been thorough, and confidence is therefore a major part of your resources, you will be able to gather the tension and excitement and use it as a truly positive force that will allow you to get the best from yourself. If you have not prepared adequately, this tension is likely to be nearer to fear than to anticipation, and only then does the condition work against you.

The amount, kind and timing of pre-race food is an important factor in race preparation. The young athlete must experiment to establish his particular likes and dislikes, but there are a few golden rules which are necessarily followed by all athletes. Eat about three hours before the race. Eat less than you would normally. Eat light, well-cooked food. And take sufficient liquid for your immediate needs, but be fairly restrained in this matter.

The interval between eating and racing is important, because the food must be properly digested without your being empty and hungry. The quantity and type of food must be intelligently judged; too much, or too heavy, food will not be cleared, and would cause a little tiredness and more than a little discomfort. The amount and type of liquid also matters, because, although it is foolish to deny the body liquid when the need is being signalled, discomfort and a 'stitch' could easily be brought about by milk among other things, or by any fluid taken in large amounts. These principles clearly apply most to races that demand sustained running. The effect of too much food or drink can, however, be drastic, even upon competitors in the shorter track events, where resulting lethargy or discomfort may affect performance.

The value of a warm-up during the half hour or so before a race is well established. It is physiologically sound to stretch the muscles, and raise the pulse rate and the general metabolism of the body as well as the body temperature, though this very slightly. This puts the whole machine through a routine which, by copying the demands to be made by the race without inducing fatigue, prepares it for its task. Not only is this physiologically sound, but the process is psychologically sound. Former world record-holder, Derek Ibbotson, pointed out that the pre-race tension lasts, 'until you start the warm-up'. Once the action starts, and the body is allowed to begin to do what the imagination has already been acting out, much of the 'nerves' evaporate. By the same token, these disappear completely when the race is under way.

Two kinds of running need to be done in the warm-up period, each achieving a special, and necessary, effect. A long period of jogging, and/or steady running ought to precede a few fast, short stretches; these are followed by continuous, relaxed jogging which takes the athlete up to the start of the race. The jogging will not tire a fit athlete, and the steady running is considerably slower than D session pace. It is accurately described as trotting, fluently, rhythmically and persistently. The short, fast stretches will barely reach 100 metres.

By this means, the whole musculature is stretched, the mind takes command of the body, the blood that has been massaged into the outposts of the muscle system is given a firm shove, with the heart pumping strongly. Again, all this is done well within the limits of acid fatigue. The final phase of easy jogging maintains the activity and the looseness up to the moment of the race. Immediately prior to the start, nothing more than walking is required, and this will allow full relaxation, and a mental gathering of forces. Most athletes also like to include some general loosening exercises in their warm-up; arm swinging, shoulder and hip rolling, high knee raising and the like are all useful and greatly recommended.

You must go to the starting line with your mind concentrated upon what is about to happen. You must be ready to take part in the *race*, however it develops. The pace set may be too fast for you, or too slow, someone may break from the field, and you will have to decide whether or not to go after him. Whatever happens, give total concentration to the race, staying fully alert, but still running fluently and without waste of energy. You are now pouring in everything that you have gathered during weeks and months of training. It would be a pity not to!

The action, and your reactions, in the early stages of a race are governed by several, mostly unpredictable, factors. The fitness and intentions of your opponents, your own exact condition, the speed at which the race is being run, are all elements in the racing situation which are only revealed gradually to you. So, although you may plan beforehand, and even have a clear idea of how you intend to run the race, it is wise to have only a flexible outline plan. You will know what to do when you are in the situation, not before. To have pitched your mind resolutely at the event, is what matters most.

The distance of the race, of course, conditions the way in which it is run. At no point in the 100 metres can there be any restraint. At no point in the 200 metres can there be any *deliberate* restraint; there is, as timings show, a very slight slackening over this distance, but it is a slackening compelled by fatigue, not followed as a plan. At and above 400 metres, intelligent control comes in. The tap that controls what is in the reservoir must be adjusted many times, so that the volume of energy released is neither too great nor too small at a given moment of the race. Going off too quickly might destroy your ability to survive at pace during the latter stages of the event, just as going off too slowly may set you adrift from your opponents and prevent you from being in at the finish. Just what speed you are able to maintain, or what is needed to win the race, must be discovered in training and racing.

It is important to remember that races are run in phases, with the tempo changing regularly. The 400 metres runner, for example, goes off at virtually maximum speed, imperceptibly eases this in the middle stages of the race, and forces every ounce out of himself round the final bend and down the straight to the finish. Running 800 metres also demands a

pace that is near to sprinting, and the athlete has to be ready
to go along with it, fighting for survival over the last couple
of hundred metres, probably with increased effort and reduced
pace. Beyond that distance, there is a vital need to get a rhythm
going, to establish a speed which it is possible to maintain.
If the pace being set is within your capability, count yourself
lucky. If it feels too fast, you must decide whether to try and
go along or to settle for a less gruelling pursuit which will
get you home, even if later than the others. It is sometimes
necessary to go beyond what you feel is sensible, in the hope
that you will surprise yourself. Mostly, as a part of your
planned progress, you will have to accept that you are not
going to win, but that you are going to stay as near to the
front as is humanly possible.

Whatever happens, in all serious racing there comes a
point, about between half and two-thirds of the way round,
when a full programme of training begins to tell, and it is at
this point, that the under-trained runner really suffers. When
discomfort builds to a nerve-grating pitch, the true athlete
is not prepared to give way; this is the very moment in the
race for which he or she has prepared. Deeply established
physical resources have been created through many months
of training, in order to take you past the point when you
would like to give up; it would be a terrible waste if you
were to do so.

'Keep your mind on the race and on your opponents, not
on your own condition.' This is the advice of Munich bronze
medallist, Ian Stewart. Of course, there are strict limits to
what the body can do, and these limits will soon be found,
though most people, runners included, will give way before
then. However, it is the runner's job to go on as long as he
can, facing positively the difficult later stages of the race and
possibly surprising himself. Ibbotson claimed never to have
finished with energy to spare when he had been beaten; he
gave all that he had because he did not want to lose.

Intelligence must again come into this, the heart of the sport. So often one sees an athlete, especially an inexperienced one, go off so fast that he has no chance at all of surviving at the pace he sets himself, with the result that he does not do himself justice. This applies to any distance and any level of competition. So, when a runner sets off at what you know to be a suicidal tempo, or breaks from the field half way through, you have to decide whether you can, or should, go with him. It is probably better to be too reckless than too careful, because recklessness is really a means of experimenting, and there will be another chance in another race, if you come unstuck.

If intelligence is a necessary element in racing, it, nevertheless, takes second place to determination. It is your character and attitude that will finally determine your chances of becoming a successful and satisfied athlete. And you do not have to reach the Olympics in order to be that; you have to know that you put in, over a long period of time, all that you could put in. It is a fine thing to be an Olympic athlete, but it is an equally fine thing to have the character of one, even if you have not got the body. Full-hearted involvement in the activity, ensuring a maximum quantity and quality of training and, therefore, the confidence which will allow you to race, this is the primary requirement. Confidence is imaginative – seeing what you can do before you do it – and if you are fully fit, and have done everything possible to prepare for the race, you will imagine that you can put in the determined effort that any race demands. With that in mind, go out and race – regularly! The training and the racing will shape your will-power into a useful instrument, which will, incidentally, help you in other spheres of your life.

At the beginning of this chapter, the difficulty of racing was touched upon. There is no doubt that the physical and mental demands of a race are enormous, whether we are considering less than a minute of 400 metres running, or more than two hours of marathon. The athlete, in either case, takes his or her resources to the contest, and there spends them. Their gathering and their distribution is a profoundly satisfying activity, as any kind of craftsmanship always is. The fact that there are few craftsmen about, should influence the young runner positively, so that he wishes to become one of that select band, who master the demanding and worthwhile craft of running.

Appendix 1

Rest and Sleep

The pattern of training must include, quite deliberately, a generous measure of rest and sleep, and it is common experience that an athlete who trains hard needs a lot of both. Exhaustion is followed by recovery, which allows more training, and during this cycle, physical improvement occurs; indeed, the second recovery phase is really part of training, and is described by the Australian swimming coach, Forbes Carlile, as a 'fundamental restorative'.

By the word 'rest', we may mean either lying down and relaxing the body without necessarily sleeping, or a respite from training on a particular day, or even during several days, as happens, for example, when an athlete is ill or injured. Many people have advised athletes to take proper rest during the day, and another Australian swimming coach, Harry Gallagher, went as far as to state that up to three hours of rest should be obtained each day, especially when, as at weekends, a heavy training load is being carried. Such advice is rarely followed, either because people who work for their living cannot find one hour, let alone three, during the day, or simply because it is not taken seriously.

Resting is more than half way towards sleeping, and it is reasonable to suppose that the profound relaxation of muscles will, in turn, remove strain from all other parts of the body, may induce the mind to close down, and must help to remove fatigue. The office worker, or the student, probably has an

93

advantage here, as so much of their day is spent sitting down; so long as the desire to fall asleep is resisted whilst work has to be done, such sitting is fairly near to proper, physical rest, and may serve as a substitute. It ought, however, to be possible to get at least a half hour of genuine rest in addition, either in the middle of the day or as soon as work has finished, and before training.

One day out of seven ought to be a rest day. This is, in the opinion of some athletes, and coaches, bad advice, but several points can be made in its defence. It is said that, if the athlete misses every Friday, then fifty-two days of training have been lost in the year. However, those days actually increase the physical capacity of the athlete to absorb, and benefit from, training. Rest, intelligently used, is part of training, for the young athlete especially. Six days of serious running (even three or four days where the very young athlete is concerned) hits the body hard, and by giving it time to absorb that amount of exercise you will ensure that it can come back for more. It must be obvious that, for example, a tough race leaves the runner tired the following day, and a series of hard training sessions such as those that have been suggested in this book, add up to a level of tiredness that may, in fact, be deeper than that of a race. Therefore, if you are training hard, give your body a chance to recover.

Take some kind of exercise on a rest day by all means, but make it a game or a walk. Feel no guilt though, if nothing much is done during the rest period. Spend some time elsewhere, enjoying another bit of life, and come back to training, eager to increase the pace, and knowing that you can do so. The young runner especially should understand that he, or she, is seeking long-term success, which results from a very protracted build-up of training. Success on the way is, of course, welcome. Success that has been planned and waited for, is even more welcome, and certain to be of a superior kind. The rest days contribute to your later success, because they keep you physically refreshed and temperamentally balanced.

Occasionally, between seasons, for example, a few days can profitably be taken away from training. Runners in Britain are going to find the last bit difficult, but the advice is sound. Coax your physical resources for a while, and get a few books into your head. What more enjoyable process could there be! Then ease back into training after this relatively slovenly episode (normal life for many people) by going for a few very long treks. Then get back to planned running, with all the renewed intention that the rest will have given you.

There are two occasions when rest is particularly important: after a really exhausting race, and when you are ill or injured. It is not often necessary to stop training completely, but it is often wise to lessen the severity or take special measures, especially in the case of injury, so that no further harm is suffered. Rest, after a serious race for middle- and long-distance runners, or after a series of races for sprinters, means carrying out light training, mostly jogging and easy running. A day or two of this should be enough to allow and assist full recovery, and should be seen as part of the training pattern.

Rest during and after illness is the only sensible conduct, and the more serious the illness, the more careful and extended should be the rest. If the body is already struggling, give it a chance, then gradually help it to pick up by building up training again. To try and maintain proper training when you are ill is brave but foolish. If you are in good condition, common illnesses will soon be thrown off. With injury, it is usually possible to continue a fair degree of training, concentrating on doing no further damage to the specific muscles involved, yet keeping yourself in generally good condition. Of course, if the injury is serious, a broken bone or torn Achilles tendon, medical help must be obtained and training may have to stop. But do not accept too readily that no exercise at all can be done. Modern physiotherapy has shown that even severely injured people can exercise other parts of their bodies, and that such exercise aids recovery.

Rest then is not a taboo word to the runner. Relaxing between hard physical and mental efforts contributes to the further advance of those efforts. In extreme cases, where there is deep exhaustion, it is only rest that will allow recuperation and, therefore, further effort. Recuperation is always a phase in the intelligent development of training. Do not let it be thought that rest should fill *too much* of the runner's routine, but make sure that the door is opened for it regularly.

Rest will often mean sleep, which is an absolute condition of overall rest. The fact that the healthy human being must sleep at least once every twenty-four hours in itself proves the total importance of this mysterious condition. Although the mechanism of sleep is not fully understood, it is a common observation that, in sleep, the processes of the body slow down and we withdraw from our surroundings, if not from ourselves. By this means, we are refreshed. Without it, the level of fatigue gradually rises to the point where it can no longer be resisted, so that we must then sleep.

If possible, do not fight against the desire to sleep. Learn a lesson from animals, though perhaps not from cats, and let go of the body when it demands release from consciousness. Then, for a few hours, the muscles relax, the waste products of fatigue are largely removed (though it may take more than one night's sleep to clear completely the acid residue of a long, hard race, or even a long, hard training session), blood perhaps comes away from the brain, the rate and volume of the heart's pumping decrease, and generally we arise fully capable of sustaining another fourteen to sixteen hours activity, including hard exercise.

There can be no hard and fast rule about the quantity of sleep which an athlete ought to take. What he or she must take is 'enough'. Franz Stampfl, who has advised such athletes as Roger Bannister and Olympic gold medallist, Ralph Doubell, said: 'Many men require ten hours if the body's resistance to the work inflicted on it is not to break down', and Harry Gallagher suggested the same amount for an athlete in full training. Ten hours is no exaggeration when the depth of tiredness and the amount of chemical fatigue arising from hard training are considered.

The most practical, intelligent approach was Ron Clarke's. He said that he aimed to go to bed early enough to ensure that he woke up without prompting. Thus, for example, if you have to get up at, say, 7 am for work or school, and having gone to bed at 11 pm you are still asleep at 7, try going at 10 pm, or 9 pm, until you find that you can wake by the necessary time without an alarm clock or a violent nudge. Another important point is to try and make the retiring and rising times regular, because experience shows that the body responds to regularity. Comfort is at the heart of the pleasure of sleeping, as well as the physical value of it as a 'restorative', so there is no need to labour the point that comfort helps proper sleep, as does peace and quiet.

Another point of concern to the athlete is early-morning running – rising straight from sleep to take fairly violent exercise, lifting the pulse rate from a minimum level to somewhere near its maximum. As with length of sleep, this is a matter for the individual to work out for himself. Some people simply cannot get up and go running almost immediately; and those who can enjoy a run before work, so long as they loosen off for an hour or so after getting up, may not have the time to do this. When a young runner has advanced to the stage where he or she wants to add a comparatively light session to the already established training-plan, he or she will have to experiment. It may be that the chance to run briefly will more easily be found at midday, or it may be that the weekend is to be used for the really thorough, double-session days. Some self-discipline is necessary, to override sluggish inclinations, in favour of an ambition to step up the training; but if you just cannot sustain and enjoy an early-morning run, assaulting sleep so violently, then this kind of effort will have to be reconsidered and as suggested, put somewhere else in the day, when the sleepy physique has been roused and loosened.

Rest and sleep, then, are vital components of training. Their contribution to racing fitness must be acknowledged, and catering for them ought to be part of all training plans. Less than a full ration of either can mean that progress is slowed.

Appendix 2

A Training Diary

Every serious athlete keeps a training diary, which is really a racing-and-training diary. A runner should record his daily training, reactions to training, any special circumstances such as illness, difficult weather conditions, exceptional degree of fatigue. He should also note race plans and details of actual races as well as the review and assessment of the current training, with comments by a coach. The diary should include a chart showing progress over given distances or courses.

The primary reason for keeping a diary is the need for as much knowledge of what you are doing as you can possibly get. As a pattern emerges from the weeks and months of training, and as this is set against a degree of success or failure in racing, it is possible to see what adjustments need to be made, what kind of training is proving most successful, and where improvement or increase can be effected. Nobody can remember the detail of training that was done some weeks earlier, unless it was recorded. Since much of the art of training, particularly as this relates to the needs of the individual, is discovered by practical experiment, it is invaluable to be able to take a long look at training which had given success, or at training which had brought little progress. So, too, matters such as over-racing, or a wrong mixture of hard training and hard racing, are quickly identified and put right when there is a diary to be read.

Perhaps more important than the details of training are the athlete's reactions to that training. It is all very well to record that '6 × 400 at good pace' was done, but it is more useful, certainly to the coach, to know whether this session put the athlete on his knees, or whether six laps at good pace were absorbed easily. If the session precedes, or follows, a race, or another particular session, then the reaction to it allows the athlete to judge combined effects. The number of practically valuable facts and ideas to be gleaned from a training diary is huge.

Adjustments to the style of training, as well as to the extent, may result from careful study of a diary also. Comments made by a runner about, say, hard sprinting sessions on a track, or long steady-paced running, will make conscious his response to these styles of exercise and allow the coach to know whether certain training is enjoyable or tedious, to be kept or changed. One session badly received means nothing, but a diary that reveals recurring dislike of a particular kind of session indicates, at least, the need to discuss that session, and improve it.

An example follows of the sort of diary that can be used. There are four basic pages: one is for details of the five different sessions planned for the individual runner; one for the daily recording of which session was done, and comments on this; one for analysis of serious or important races; and a progress chart on which is entered a list of improving times for the chosen race distance, as well as a note of who won races over particular courses and what the course record is (obviously, more relevant to distance runners than to sprinters or middle-distance runners). On the progress chart, it is best to enter only improved times, as this will create an extra incentive.

When, at a given point in a season, adjustments are made to the training-pattern, the first sheet of these four is rewritten. In this way, all seasonal changes are noted, and the new pattern is found before the pages which record how it is carried out. For example, a winter's training plan may be found on a late-September sheet, and the pages covering, say, September–December reveal how this plan was pursued.

Race analysis

1 **Venue:** Maidstone
   Time: 21·12   **Position:** 5th
   Winner's name: A. Newman
   Winner's time: 20·31

Date: 10 February 1974
Distance: 3½ miles

**Own best time
   to date:**

---

2 **Number of hours sleep night before:** nine plus

---

3 **Food eaten before race, and when:** cereal, toast – 3hrs before

---

4 **Type of warm-up carried out:** 10min jogging, couple of strides

---

5 **Tactics in early stages of race:** not too bothered – went with main pack

---

6 **At what point discomfort set in:** felt pretty good all way – not taking it too
                                         seriously!

---

7 **Whether absolutely maximum effort was made:** not really – save it for
                                                    summer

---

8 **How long it took to recover:**
   (a) from immediate exhaustion: felt all right within 10 mins
   (b) completely: next day, except bit of local stiffness

---

9 **What can be learned from this race:** wait for the track! enjoyed it though
                                            and it makes good D session

---

10 **Next race:** Southern Counties' winter meeting 400m in about ten days'
                    time

Week ending 10 February	**Week ending** 17 February
Sunday kept going **C** beyond hour, as felt good	**Sunday** **C** and **E**
Monday hard session **A** with good pace	**Monday** very cold, could **A** not get going
Tuesday not able to **B** sprint much, as conditions bad	**Tuesday** did D session as **D** feeling tired after heavy week last week and c-c race
Wednesday good session **A** on track	**Wednesday** fairly good session **A** on track – timed the 200s
Thursday went on the **D** country – good session and maintained pace	**Thursday** track again, and **B** some hills away from track – long easy run home
Friday	**Friday**
Saturday school cross-country **D** match, finished 5th	**Saturday** went with club boys, **C** good long session
Race details:	**Race details:**

Observations for this fortnight:

Kept fairly good pattern going, but had to change plans a bit once or twice. Feel very fit and can do all sessions without too much strain. Cannot keep them going, though, for more than about five or six in sequence.

A   20min steady running; 3 × 300; 3 × 200; 10–15min easy running with short bursts

B   (as conditions allow) 20min steady; series of short, hard hill runs; 10min easy; series of short, hard sprints; easy running to finish

C   trek for about an hour, mixing many short fast stretches with jogging and running easily

D   steady paced run up to 5 miles – good, fluent run

E   relaxed run for 2 to 3 miles when possible, especially at weekends

PROGRESS CHART

Year: 1974

Racing distance:	200m	400m	800m		
Track personal best bt. f'ward	24·8	53·4	1·59		
		53·2			

Established courses
(road/c–country)

school course

best: 21·24

1974:

Camberley R.R.

best: 6·50

1974:

Thurrock R.R.

best: 5·40

1974:

Appendix 3

Equipment

Equipment should be carefully chosen and maintained. Shoes, socks, shorts, vests, and tracksuits are necessary items on the runner's list. Sprinters also need starting blocks, and most athletes eventually like to have their own stop-watch.

There are four kinds of shoe – road, spike, stud and ripple. Within these categories, the range of styling, quality and price is considerable, but heavy spending is always justified, because a lot of injury can derive from ill-protected feet and legs. Twice the price is half the trouble in the long run.

Your priority purchase should be a pair of road shoes by one of the leading makers, with a good sole and well-padded uppers. Nylon uppers ensure a light shoe, though the nylon can prove troublesome in hot weather when trapped warmth easily creates blisters. A shoe made from animal skin is best. A good sole is not necessarily thick; modern running shoes often have a sponge layer inserted between a thin, tough sole and the upper, so that ample protection is given, without need for a thick, and probably heavy, sole. Road shoes can be carefully 'broken in' if they are worn like a slipper around the house for a few hours. In this way, they will settle gradually and thoroughly on to the feet.

All but the cheapest track running shoes will have screw-in spikes, allowing short 'needle' spikes to be inserted for use on all-weather tracks, and the slightly longer spike when you are competing on grass, or on the old-fashioned marl surface. Spiked shoes are very light and must be so, with a glove fitting and, preferably, some protection under the heel. A good pair for racing is necessary. Like your road shoes, these spikes will be expensive but will be a sound investment. Always remove the spikes during months when there may be no track competition, and put a dob of vaseline in the holes. If this is done, the spikes will always be removable without difficulty.

For cross-country, where the ground does not allow either road shoes or spikes successfully to be worn, studs or ripples are required. Neither is a totally adequate shoe, however. On a largely road-run course, studs will soon be spoiled and ripples do not have sufficient heel protection against hard surfaces, and may admit injury. The ripple-soled shoe is, though, a useful piece of equipment for cross-country running and affords good grip except down hill. The soles last a long time and the answer to heel protection lies in the choice of training ground; slower running can be done where stretches of road are encountered. Jarring of legs is thus, to a large extent, avoided. For cross-country racing, studs are preferable. In any case, try to inspect a course beforehand, so that you can decide which shoes to use. Modern cross-country is often held over grassland and spikes can be worn there. Incidentally, take a newspaper to cross-country races! Muddy shoes can then be wrapped.

Blisters can be avoided by putting a smear of Vaseline on toes and heels. Infections such as verruca and 'athletes foot' will be less of a hazard if the runner has a small square of hard nylon matting for standing on and if this is washed regularly. Remember, too, to carry spare laces. A lace inevitably breaks at the crucial moment.

Socks with nylon-reinforced soles will complete a runner's foot comfort and protection, and will survive hard wear, especially if toe nails are cut weekly.

Shorts should fit comfortably and allow complete freedom

of movement. Boys and men should always wear a supporter strap. Vests also ought to be exactly the right size. Cotton vests are superior to nylon, because in hot weather nylon is extremely uncomfortable when sweat builds up inside. It is a good idea to have a clean vest in reserve if you are contesting preliminary rounds and a final on the same day; qualify for the final, then have a quick shower and put on the clean garment. You will feel refreshed.

Obviously, all athletes need a tracksuit, and nylon is best because it is light and protective. If needed in training, a T-shirt or windcheater top is a practical substitute for the tracksuit top. There is no point in spoiling an expensive tracksuit, which should be kept for pre-competition use. For really bad weather, a special nylon top can be obtained, similar to a ski anorak.

The wrist band used by tennis players is also useful during lengthy training sessions and longer distance races, when some relief from sweat is welcome. After a season or two, the young runner may want to own a stop-watch, to confirm training efforts and provide incentive. Use the stop-watch intelligently; it is a valuable indicator but too easily becomes an obsession.

The sprinter needs his own starting-blocks, plus nails and a hammer, and perhaps a measuring tape to check the alignment of blocks. It may begin to appear that a runner must carry a formidable burden of equipment! But modern blocks are light and the rest of the equipment is easily packed into a hold-all.

Finally, all of this equipment should be checked before you travel. There are few things more aggravating to an athlete than to be in the dressing room and to discover that an essential piece of kit has been left at home.

Appendix 4

Where to Find Help

To progress in athletics, it is necessary to join a good club, find an adult who will help you with your training and racing and keep gathering knowledge – from books, magazines, mixing with athletes, and going on training courses.

Almost everywhere in Britain, there is an athletics club within reach of the determined and ambitious young runner. Within the boundaries of the more populous English counties, there may be ten or more, so you should not have to travel more than twenty miles or so to find one. That does not mean that the one you find is always a good one; so it is sensible to get to know something about a club before you decide to join it. While an athlete is at school, then the school has the first claim on his participation anyway, so that membership of a club is not strongly binding, and if the athlete is unhappy as a member, membership may be resigned without any complications upon leaving school, and new, 'first-claim' membership taken up. (The details of this matter of membership can be found in the *BAAB Handbook*, or obtained from your Area or County Association). Whatever the situation, the important thing is to join a club, and to begin both to use and to help that club. Your running will be better for it, and the more young people who join clubs, the stronger the sport will be everywhere. If there isn't a club in your area, as might be the case, then get together with other people, of all ages, and start one!

What you should look for in a club is enthusiasm, good organisation, good facilities (especially in your event), a full fixture list, coaching and, according to your taste, an interesting social life. Very few clubs will be able to offer a completely satisfying measure of these things, but they ought all to be there in some degree.

It will not take you long to sense whether the club is enthusiastic and well organised, because you can gauge both the atmosphere and the organisation as soon as you take part in a fixture. Enthusiastic athletes talk about their competitions, their training, their ambitions and their club. Well organised clubs notify members, in good time, of the details of time and travel, and make sure that somebody contacts a new member, speaks with him, and keeps the member informed of future events, offering help at all times, and being able to provide it once it has been accepted.

The facilities a club offers are important, though their importance could be overrated. Without the basic facilities, such as adequate changing rooms, an available track, and equipment for field events, no club can thrive; but athletes have reached Olympic level without the aid of all-weather tracks or private massage. What matters to the young athlete, once he finds a club that does actually have a club-house and a ground, is the noticeable desire of that club to help and encourage its members, and to be looking for improvement. Of course, many British clubs, especially in London, Birmingham, Edinburgh and other cities, have obtained first-class facilities, and are probably better for it. But all that glitters is not necessarily gold; Mary Peters and Buster McShane proved what could be done when circumstances were not wholly favourable. Still, it is as well to look for a club with a lot to offer, remembering always that it is what you have to offer that will eventually bring success.

It is very important that the club you join should have a full, strong fixture list, including all of the county, area and

109

national championships. Local club matches are enjoyable and are part of the sport, but you need to know that you will be able to measure yourself, step by step, against runners who are better than you. This is especially important for the sprinters who are also part of relay squads, and the distance runners who nearly always find themselves in team events. Plan your progress along the line of an ambitious fixture list.

Most of the necessary coaching will be available from a good club, though you may wish to contact an individual coach, through the club, for specialist training, in, for example, sprinting. Usually, it is to everyone's advantage that an athlete should get his coaching from within the club. This prevents split loyalty and strengthens coaching groups within clubs.

Help and advice should never be scorned. Talk with those who seem to know about training and racing. If you find somebody whose knowledge and enthusiasm convince you, then join with him, or her. Not many coaches will approach an athlete first; you will have to be bold enough to ask, and then you will always get a warm response. Remember, too, that the adult coach will judge your level of enthusiasm, your serious desire to train hard and regularly, and also that he has other business to attend to, a living to earn, and usually a house and family to look after. This means that you have to be reliable, and not waste a coach's time and efforts. The partnership of coach and athlete can be a very interesting, enjoyable and satisfying one for both parties, provided there is willingness from both sides. It may start out as a sporting association and end up a strong friendship, especially when the older person is not wearing blinkers, but has interests and knowledge beyond the running track.

A country which takes its athletics seriously – and Britain, on the whole, deserves inclusion here – will have County and Area Associations that regularly put on instruction and training courses for young athletes. These same valuable courses are regularly arranged by clubs and, in the most progressive places, by county school associations. These courses may be one-day affairs, or week-end residential occasions (as at the Crystal Palace National Recreation Centre), or may even last for a week or more. An ambitious young athlete would be well advised to join one, because time spent with other keen, and probably talented, runners is time profitably spent; enthusiasm increases, knowledge is gathered, and hard training is done in the best possible circumstances. You are unlikely to come away from an organised course without a feeling that you want to intensify your efforts.

Although training courses are not widely advertised, their existence can always be discovered through a club, or directly from the nationally distributed magazine, *Athletics Weekly*, which almost always has this kind of information, and should, incidentally, become part of your regular reading. This, and a selection from the hundreds of book and magazines that have been published on the subject of running, is detailed below in the belief that a young runner will enjoy reading about the sport and keeping up to date with what happens in it. The magazines will provide current news, comment, training articles and so on. The books mentioned, will give full technical information, examples of the training done by top men and women, and, often, a valuable insight into the character of those top athletes. A good many of the books are unfortunately no longer in print, and cannot therefore be bought, but most of them will be found in local libraries.

Bibliography

MAGAZINES

Athletics Weekly, published from 344 High Street, Rochester, Kent

Athletics in Scotland, published from 7 Durham Square, Edinburgh

Runner's World, published from PO Box 366, Mountain View, California 94040, and obtainable from PO Box 247, Croydon, Surrey

Track and Field News, published from PO Box 296, Los Altos, California 94022, and obtainable from *Athletics Weekly*

BOOKS

AAA. *Amateur Athletic Association Handbook (Part Two: Rules for Competition)* AAA, 70 Brompton Road, London SW3 1EE, published annually

Bannister, Roger. *First Four Minutes* (Putnam, 1955)

Cerrutty, Percy. *Athletics: How to Become a Champion* (Stanley Paul, 1960)

——. *Middle Distance Running* (Pelham, 1964)

——. *Schoolboy Athletics* (Stanley Paul, 1963)

Clarke, Ron. *The Lonely Breed* (Pelham, 1967)

——. *The Unforgiving Minute* (Pelham, 1966)

Elliott, Herb. *The Golden Mile* (Cassell, 1961)

113

Emery, David. *Lillian* (Hodder & Stoughton, 1971)

Gilmour, Garth. *A Clean Pair of Heels* (Herbert Jenkins, 1964)

Harris, Norman. *The Legend of Lovelock* (Kaye, 1965)

Henderson, Joe (ed). *Guide to Distance Running* (Runner's World Publications, 1971)

——. *The Complete Runner* (Runner's World Publications, 1974)

Hyman, Dorothy. *Sprint to Fame* (Stanley Paul, 1964)

Karpovich, Peter and Sinning, Wayne. *Physiology of Muscular Activity* (Sanders, 1971)

Lovesey, Peter. *Kings of Distance* (Eyre & Spottiswoode, 1968)

Lydiard, Arthur. *Run to the Top* (Herbert Jenkins, 1968)

Marlow, Bill and Watts, Denis. *Track Athletics* (Pelham, 1970)

Masurier, John Le. *Track Speed* (Stanley Paul, 1972)

Mitchell, Brian. *Athletics Through the Looking Glass* (Wildlife and Country Photos, 1972)

——. *Today's Athlete* (Pelham, 1970)

National Union of Track Statisticians. *Athletics (UK) Annual* (NUTS, 78 Toynbee Road, London SW20 8SR)

Nelson, Bert. *The Jim Ryun Story* (Pelham, 1968)

Peters, Mary and Woolridge, Ian. *Mary P* (Stanley Paul, 1974)

Pirie, Gordon. *Running Wild* (Allen & Unwin, 1961)

Snell, Peter. *No Bugles, No Drums* (Hodder & Stoughton, 1966)

Stampfl, Franz. *On Running* (Herbert Jenkins, 1955)

Temple, Cliff (ed). *Cross-Country Running for Girls* (Women's CC Association, 1973)

Tulloh, Bruce. *Tulloh on Running* (Heinemann, 1968)

Tulloh, Bruce and Hyman, Martin. *Long Distance Running* (AAA, 1966)

Ward, Tony. *Modern Distance Running* (Stanley Paul, 1964)

Watman, Melvyn. *Encyclopaedia of Athletics* (Robert Hale, 1974

Watts, Denis; Wilson, Harry and Horwill, Frank. *The Complete Middle Distance Runner* (Stanley Paul, 1972)

Wilt, Fred. *How They Train* (Track and Field News, 1973)

———. *Run Run Run* (Track and Field News, 1974)

Woodeson, Peggy and Watts, Denis. *Schoolgirl Athletics* (Stanley Paul, 1966)

Index